Fremdsprachentexte

John Millington Synge

The Playboy of the Western World

Herausgegeben von
Rainer Lengeler

Philipp Reclam jun. Stuttgart

Universal-Bibliothek Nr. 9211 [2]
Alle Rechte vorbehalten
© 1986 Philipp Reclam jun., Stuttgart
Gesamtherstellung: Reclam, Ditzingen
Printed in Germany 1986
ISBN 3-15-009211-6

Preface

In writing *The Playboy of the Western World*, as in my
other plays, I have used one or two words only, that I
have not heard among the country people of Ireland, or
spoken in my own nursery before I could read the
newspapers. A certain number of the phrases I employ I
have heard also from herds and fishermen along the
coast from Kerry to Mayo, or from beggar-women and
ballad-singers nearer Dublin; and I am glad to acknow-
ledge how much I owe to the folk-imagination of these
fine people. Anyone who has lived in real intimacy with
the Irish peasantry will know that the wildest sayings
and ideas in this play are tame indeed compared with
the fancies one may hear in any little hillside cabin in
Geesala, or Carraroe, or Dingle Bay. All art is a collaboration; and there is little doubt that in the happy
ages of literature striking and beautiful phrases were as
ready to the story-teller's or the playwright's hand as the
rich cloaks and dresses of his time. It is probable that
when the Elizabethan dramatist took his ink-horn and

---

7 **herd** (dial.): Hirt.
12 **peasantry:** Landvolk, Bauern.
13 **tame:** zahm.
14 **cabin:** Hütte.
15 **Geesala / Carraroe / Dingle Bay:** Örtlichkeiten im Westen Irlands,
die Synge auch in seinen Reisebeschreibungen erwähnt. Geesala auf
der Halbinsel Erris liegt im äußersten Nordwesten, Carraroe auf der
Höhe von Galway und die Dingle Bay in der Grafschaft Kerry im
Südwesten.
15 f. **collaboration:** Zusammenarbeit.
18 **playwright:** Schauspieldichter, Bühnenschriftsteller.
20 **ink-horn:** Tintenhorn, Tintenfaß.

sat down to his work he used many phrases that he had
just heard, as he sat at dinner, from his mother or his
children. In Ireland those of us who know the people
have the same privilege. When I was writing *The Shad-*
5 *ow of the Glen*, some years ago, I got more aid than any
learning could have given me, from a chink in the floor
of the old Wicklow house where I was staying, that let
me hear what was being said by the servant girls in the
kitchen. This matter, I think, is of importance, for in
10 countries where the imagination of the people, and the
language they use, is rich and living, it is possible for a
writer to be rich and copious in his words, and at the
same time to give the reality which is the root of all
poetry, in a comprehensive and natural form. In the
15 modern literature of towns, however, richness is found
only in sonnets, or prose poems, or in one or two
elaborate books that are far away from the profound
and common interests of life. One has, on one side,
Mallarmé and Huysmans producing this literature; and
20 on the other Ibsen and Zola dealing with the reality of
life in joyless and pallid words. On the stage one must
have reality, and one must have joy, and that is why the
intellectual modern drama has failed, and people have

---

5 **glen:** Bergtal.
6 **chink:** Spalt.
12 **copious:** wortreich.
14 **comprehensive:** umfassend, weit.
16 **sonnet:** Sonett (Gedichtform).
17 **elaborate:** kompliziert, gekünstelt.
19/20 **Mallarmé / Huysmans / Ibsen / Zola:** Stéphane M. (1842–98),
   französischer Dichter; Joris-Karl H. (1848–1907), französischer
   Schriftsteller; Henrik I. (1828–1906), norwegischer Schriftsteller;
   Emile Z. (1840–1902), französischer Schriftsteller.
21 **pallid:** blaß, bleich.

grown sick of the false joy of the musical comedy, that has been given them in place of the rich joy found only in what is superb and wild in reality. In a good play every speech should be as fully flavoured as a nut or
5 apple, and such speeches cannot be written by anyone who works among people who have shut their lips on poetry. In Ireland, for a few years more, we have a popular imagination that is fiery and magnificent, and tender; so that those of us who wish to write start with a
10 chance that is not given to writers in places where the springtime of the local life has been forgotten, and the harvest is a memory only, and the straw has been turned into bricks.

January 21st, 1907   *J. M. S.*

3 **superb:** herrlich, prächtig.
4 **to flavour:** würzen, duften.

The Playboy
of the Western World

Persons

CHRISTOPHER MAHON
OLD MAHON, his father, a squatter
MICHAEL JAMES FLAHERTY (called Michael James), a publican
MARGARET FLAHERTY (called Pegeen Mike), his daughter
SHAWN KEOGH, her second cousin, a young farmer
PHILLY O'CULLEN ⎫
JIMMY FARRELL ⎭ small farmers
WIDOW QUIN
SARA TANSEY ⎫
SUSAN BRADY ⎪
HONOR BLAKE ⎬ village girls
NELLY MCLAUGHLIN ⎭
A BELLMAN
SOME PEASANTS

Scene

The action takes place near a village, on a wild coast of Mayo. The first Act passes on a dark evening of autumn, the other two Acts on the following day.

---

3 **squatter:** Ansiedler ohne Rechtstitel.
4 f. **publican:** Gastwirt.
16 **bellman:** Ausrufer.

Act I

Country public house or shebeen, very rough and untidy.
There is a sort of counter on the right with shelves,
holding many bottles and jugs, just seen above it. Empty
barrels stand near the counter. At back, a little to left of
counter, there is a door into the open air; then, more to
the left, there is a settle with shelves above it, with more
jugs, and a table beneath a window. At the left there is a
large open fire-place, with turf fire, and a small door into
inner room. Pegeen, a wild-looking but fine girl of about
twenty, is writing at table. She is dressed in the usual
peasant dress.

PEGEEN (*slowly, as she writes*). Six yards of stuff for
   to make a yellow gown. A pair of lace boots with
   lengthy heels on them and brassy eyes. A hat is suited
   for a wedding-day. A fine tooth comb. To be sent
   with three barrels of porter in Jimmy Farrell's creel

---

 2 **shebeen** (ir.): billige Straßenschenke.
 4 **jug:** Krug.
 7 **settle:** Holzbank mit Lehne.
 9 **turf:** Torf.
14 **gown:** Kleid.
   lace boot: Schnürstiefel (*to lace:* schnüren).
14 f. **with lengthy heels:** mit hohen Absätzen.
15 **brassy eye:** Metallöse.
17 **porter:** Abk. für *porter's ale:* tief dunkelbraunes, alkoholreiches
   obergäriges Bier.
17 f. **creel cart:** Karren, dessen Aufbau aus Weidengeflecht besteht.

cart on the evening of the coming Fair to Mister
Michael James Flaherty. With the best compliments
of this season: Margaret Flaherty.

SHAWN KEOGH *(a fat and fair young man comes in down*
5   *right centre as she signs and looks round awkwardly,*
when he sees she is alone). Where's himself?

PEGEEN *(without looking at him).* He's coming. *(She*
directs letter.) To Mister Sheamus Mulroy, Wine and
Spirit Dealer, Castlebar.

10   SHAWN *(uneasily).* I didn't see him on the road.

PEGEEN. How would you see him *(licks stamp and puts it*
on letter) and it dark night this half an hour gone by?

SHAWN *(turning towards door again).* I stood a while
outside wondering would I have a right to pass on or
15   to walk in and see you, Pegeen Mike *(comes to the*
fire), and I could hear the cows breathing, and sighing
in the stillness of the air, and not a step moving any
place from this gate to the bridge.

PEGEEN *(putting letter in envelope).* It's above at the
20   cross-roads he is, meeting Philly O'Cullen and a
couple more are going along with him to Kate Cassidy's wake.

SHAWN *(looking at her blankly).* And he's going that
length in the dark night?

25   PEGEEN *(impatiently).* He is surely, and leaving me lonesome on the scruff of the hill. *(She gets up and puts*
envelope on dresser, then winds clock.) Isn't it long

1 **fair:** Jahrmarkt.
8 **to direct:** adressieren.
22 **wake:** Totenwache, die häufig in Besäufnisse ausartet.
23 **blankly** (adv.): starr, erstaunt.
26 **scruff:** hier: Hang (unterhalb des Gipfels).
27 **dresser:** Anrichte.

the nights are now, Shawn Keogh, to be leaving a
poor girl with her own self counting the hours to the
dawn of day?

SHAWN *(with awkward humour)*. If it is, when we're
5 wedded in a short while you'll have no call to com-
plain, for I've little will to be walking off to wakes
or weddings in the darkness of the night.

PEGEEN *(with rather scornful good humour)*. You're
making mighty certain, Shaneen, that I'll wed you
10 now.

SHAWN. Aren't we after making a good bargain, the way
we're only waiting these days on Father Reilly's
dispensation from the bishops or the Court of Rome.

PEGEEN *(looking at him teasingly, washing up at dresser)*.
15 It's a wonder, Shaneen, the Holy Father'd be taking
notice of the likes of you, for if I was him, I wouldn't
bother with this place where you'll meet none but
Red Linahan, has a squint in his eye, and Patcheen is
lame in his heel, or the mad Mulrannies were driven
20 from California and they lost in their wits. We're a
queer lot these times to go troubling the Holy Father
on his sacred seat.

SHAWN *(scandalized)*. If we are, we're as good this place

---

5 **no call to:** keine Veranlassung.
8 **scornful:** verächtlich.
13 **dispensation:** kirchlicher Dispens, der für die Heirat zwischen Ver-
wandten erforderlich war.
14 **teasingly** (adv.): neckend, neckisch, hänselnd (*to tease:* necken,
hänseln).
18 **squint:** Schielen, schielender Blick.
21 **queer:** sonderbar.
lot: Haufen, Sippschaft.
23 **scandalized:** empört, Anstoß nehmend.

as another, maybe, and as good these times as we
were for ever.

PEGEEN *(with scorn)*. As good, is it? Where now will you
meet the like of Daneen Sullivan knocked the eye
5 from a peeler, or Marcus Quin, God rest him, got six
months for maiming ewes, and he a great warrant to
tell stories of holy Ireland till he'd have the old
women shedding down tears about their feet. Where
will you find the like of them, I'm saying?

10 SHAWN *(timidly)*. If you don't, it's a good job, maybe,
for *(with peculiar emphasis on the words)* Father
Reilly has small conceit to have that kind walking
around and talking to the girls.

PEGEEN *(impatiently, throwing water from basin out of*
15   *the door)*. Stop tormenting me with Father Reilly
(imitating his voice), when I'm asking only what way
I'll pass these twelve hours of dark, and not take my
death with the fear. *(Looking out of door.)*

SHAWN *(timidly)*. Would I fetch you the Widow Quin,
20   maybe.

PEGEEN. Is it the like of that murderer? You'll not, surely.

SHAWN *(going to her, soothingly)*. Then I'm thinking

---

3 **scorn:** Verachtung.
5 **peeler:** Schutzmann (nach dem britischen Staatsmann Sir Robert
Peel [1788–1850]).
6 **to maim:** verstümmeln.
  ewe: Mutterschaf.
6f. **he a great warrant to tell stories:** etwa: er versteht sich aufs Er-
zählen *(warrant:* Garant).
11 **emphasis:** Nachdruck.
12 **to have small conceit:** wenig schätzen, eine geringe Meinung haben
(conceit: Vorliebe).

himself will stop along with you when he sees you
taking on, for it'll be a long night and with great
darkness, and I'm after feeling a kind of fellow above
in the furzy ditch, groaning wicked like a maddening
5   dog, the way it's good cause you have, maybe, to be
fearing now.

PEGEEN (*turning on him sharply*). What's that? Is it a
man you seen?

SHAWN (*retreating*). I couldn't see him at all, but I heard
10   him groaning out and breaking his heart. It should
have been a young man from his words speaking.

PEGEEN (*going after him*). And you never went near to
see was he hurted or what ailed him at all?

SHAWN. I did not, Pegeen Mike. It was a dark lonesome
15   place to be hearing the like of him.

PEGEEN. Well, you're a daring fellow! And if they find
his corpse stretched above in the dews of dawn,
what'll you say then to the peelers or the Justice of
the Peace?

20 SHAWN (*thunderstruck*). I wasn't thinking of that. For
the love of God, Pegeen Mike, don't let on I was
speaking of him. Don't tell your father and the men is
coming above, for if they heard that story they'd have
great blabbing this night at the wake.

25 PEGEEN. I'll maybe tell them, and I'll maybe not.

---

2 **to take on:** sich aufregen, sich sorgen.
3 **and I'm after feeling a kind of fellow:** wo ich doch eben einen Kerl
bemerkt habe.
4 **furzy:** voll von Stechginster (*furze:* Stechginster).
4f. **maddening dog:** tollwütiger Hund.
13 **to ail:** unwohl sein, fehlen.
21 **to let on** (infml.): (ver)petzen.
24 **blabbing:** Geschwätz.

SHAWN. They are coming at the door. Will you whisht,
I'm saying.

PEGEEN. Whisht yourself.

(She goes behind counter. Michael James, fat jovial
5 *publican, comes in down right centre followed by*
Philly O'Cullen, who is thin and mistrusting, and
Jimmy Farrell, who is fat and amorous, about forty-
five.)

MEN *(together)*. God bless you. The blessing of God on
10 this place.

PEGEEN. God bless you kindly.

MICHAEL *(to men, who go to the counter right)*. Sit down
now, and take your rest. *(Crosses to Shawn at the fire*
left.) And how is it you are, Shawn Keogh? Are you
15 coming over the sands to Kate Cassidy's wake?

SHAWN. I am not, Michael James. I'm going home the
short-cut to my bed.

PEGEEN *(speaking across from counter)*. He's right too,
and have you no shame, Michael James, to be quit-
20 ting off for the whole night and leaving myself lonesome in the shop?

MICHAEL *(good-humouredly)*. Isn't it the same whether I
go for the whole night or a part only? and I'm
thinking it's a queer daughter you are if you'd have
25 me crossing backward through the Stooks of the
Dead Women, with a drop taken.

---

1 **to whisht:** still sein; pst machen.
4 **jovial:** leutselig.
7 **amorous:** verliebt.
19 f. **to quit off:** sich davonscheren.
22 **good-humouredly** (adv.): gut gelaunt.
25 f. **Stooks of the Dead Women:** Küstenfelsen, die wie Garben ausse-
hen und von denen die Sage geht, daß dort ein Boot mit zwölf toten
Frauen gelandet sei.

PEGEEN *(angrily)*. If I am a queer daughter, it's a queer father'd be leaving me lonesome these twelve hours of dark, and I piling the turf with the dogs barking, and the calves mooing, and my own teeth rattling with the fear.

JIMMY *(flatteringly)*. What is there to hurt you and you a fine, hardy girl would knock the head of any two men in the place.

PEGEEN *(working herself up)*. Isn't there the harvest boys with their tongues red for drink, and the ten tinkers is camped in the east glen, and the thousand militia – bad cess to them! – walking idle through the land? There's lots surely to hurt me, and I won't stop alone in it, let himself do what he will.

MICHAEL. If you're that afeard, let Shawn Keogh stop along with you. It's the will of God, I'm thinking, himself should be seeing to you now. *(They all turn on Shawn.)*

SHAWN *(in horrified confusion)*. I would and welcome, Michael James; but I'm afeard of Father Reilly, and what at all would the Holy Father and the Cardinals of Rome be saying if they heard I did the like of that?

MICHAEL *(with contempt)*. God help you! Can't you sit in by the hearth with the light lit and herself beyond in the room? You'll do that surely, for I've heard tell there's a queer fellow above going mad or getting his

---

3 **to pile:** stapeln, sammeln.
11 **tinker:** Kesselflicker.
12 **militia:** Miliz, Bürgerwehr; hier: Milizsoldat.
   cess: Abk. für *success* (ir.): unglückliches Ende.
19 **I would and welcome:** ich würde es und das gerne (tun).
22f. **the like of that:** so etwas.

death, maybe, in the gripe of the ditch, so she'd be
safer this night with a person here.

SHAWN *(with plaintive despair)*. I'm afeard of Father
Reilly, I'm saying. Let you not be tempting me and
5 we near married itself.

PHILLY *(with cold contempt)*. Lock him in the west room.
He'll stay then and have no sin to be telling to the
priest.

MICHAEL *(to Shawn, getting between him and the door)*.
10 Go up now.

SHAWN *(at the top of his voice)*. Don't stop me, Michael
James. Let me out of the door, I'm saying, for the
love of the Almighty God. Let me out *(trying to
dodge past him)*. Let me out of it and may God grant
15 you His indulgence in the hour of need.

MICHAEL *(loudly)*. Stop your noising and sit down by
the hearth. *(Gives him a push and goes to counter
laughing.)*

SHAWN *(turning back, wringing his hands)*. Oh, Father
20 Reilly and the saints of God, where will I hide myself
today? Oh, St. Joseph and St. Patrick and St. Brigid
and St. James, have mercy on me now! *(He turns
round, sees door clear and makes a rush for it.)*

MICHAEL *(catching him by the coat-tail)*. You'd be going,
25 is it?

SHAWN *(screaming)*. Leave me go, Michael James, leave

---

1 **gripe** (= *grip*; dial.): kleiner Graben, Rinne.
3 **plaintive:** weinerlich.
14 **to dodge:** schlüpfen.
15 **indulgence:** Vergebung.
19 **to wring:** umdrehen, ringen.
21 **St. Brigid:** Brigitte von Kildare, Patronin der Iren.
23 **to make a rush for s.th.:** sich auf etwas stürzen.
24 **coat-tail:** Rockschoß.

me go, you old Pagan, leave me go or I'll get the
curse of the priests on you, and of the scarlet-coated
bishops of the courts of Rome. *(With a sudden movement he pulls himself out of his coat and disappears
out of the door, leaving his coat in Michael's hands.)*

MICHAEL *(turning round, and holding up coat)*. Well,
there's the coat of a Christian man. Oh, there's
sainted glory this day in the lonesome west, and by
the will of God I've got you a decent man, Pegeen,
you'll have no call to be spying after if you've a score
of young girls, maybe, weeding in your fields.

PEGEEN *(taking up the defence of her property)*. What
right have you to be making game of a poor fellow for
minding the priest when it's your own fault is, not
paying a penny pot-boy to stand along with me and
give me courage in the doing of my work? *(She snaps
the coat away from him, and goes behind counter with
it.)*

MICHAEL *(taken aback)*. Where would I get a pot-boy?
Would you have me send the bell-man screaming in
the streets of Castlebar?

SHAWN *(opening the door a chink and putting in his head,
in a small voice)*. Michael James!

---

 1 **pagan:** Heide.
 2 **scarlet-coated:** im scharlachroten Gewand.
 9 **decent:** anständig, gesittet.
10 **score:** zwanzig (Stück).
11 **to weed:** Unkraut jäten.
13 **to make game of s.o.:** jdn. aufziehen, zum besten haben.
14 **to mind s.o.:** auf jdn. hören.
15 **penny pot-boy:** Bierkellner.
16f. **to snap away:** weg-, entreißen.
19 **taken aback:** überrascht, entgeistert.
23 **in a small voice:** mit leiser, sanfter Stimme.

MICHAEL *(imitating him)*. What ails you?

SHAWN. The queer dying fellow's beyond looking over
the ditch. He's come up, I'm thinking, stealing your
hens. *(Looks over his shoulder.)* God help me, he's
5   following me now *(he runs into room)*, and if he's
heard what I said, he'll be having my life and I going
home lonesome in the darkness of the night.

*(For a perceptible moment they watch the door with
curiosity. Someone coughs outside. Then Christy Ma-*
10   *hon, a slight young man, comes in, very tired and
frightened and dirty.)*

CHRISTY *(in a small voice)*. God save all here!

MEN. God save you kindly.

CHRISTY *(going to counter)*. I'd trouble you for a glass of
15   porter, woman of the house. *(He puts down coin.)*

PEGEEN *(serving him)*. You're one of the tinkers, young
fellow, is beyond camped in the glen?

CHRISTY. I am not; but I'm destroyed walking.

MICHAEL *(patronizingly)*. Let you come up then to the
20   fire. You're looking famished with the cold.

CHRISTY. God reward you. *(He takes up his glass, and
goes a little way across to the left, then stops and looks
about him.)* Is it often the polis do be coming into this
place, master of the house?

25   MICHAEL. If you'd come in better hours, you'd have seen
"Licensed for the Sale of Beer and Spirits, to be

---

8 **for a perceptible moment:** für einen merklichen Augenblick.
10 **slight:** dünn, schmächtig.
18 **I'm destroyed walking:** ich bin hin, kaputt vom Gehen.
19 **patronizingly** (adv.): gönnerhaft.
20 **to famish:** aushungern.
21 **to reward:** vergelten, lohnen.
23 **polis:** Polente.

consumed on the Premises", written in white letters
above the door, and what would the polis want spying
on me, and not a decent house within four miles, the
way every living Christian is a bona fide saving one
5 widow alone?

CHRISTY *(with relief)*. It's a safe house, so. *(He goes over
to the fire, sighing and moaning. Then he sits down
putting his glass beside him and begins gnawing a
turnip, too miserable to feel the others staring at him
10 with curiosity.)*

MICHAEL *(going after him)*. Is it yourself is fearing the
polis? You're wanting, maybe?

CHRISTY. There's many wanting.

MICHAEL. Many surely, with the broken harvest and the
15 ended wars. *(He picks up some stockings etc. that are
near the fire, and carries them away furtively.)* It
should be larceny, I'm thinking?

CHRISTY *(dolefully)*. I had it in my mind it was a different
word and a bigger.

20 PEGEEN. There's a queer lad! Were you never slapped in

---

1 **to consume:** verzehren, verbrauchen.
  on the premises: eigtl.: auf dem Grundstück; hier: am Schankort, an
  Ort und Stelle.
4 **bona fide:** Abk. für *bona fide traveller:* wirklicher Reisender, für den
  die Schankzeiten nicht gelten.
  saving: außer.
6 **relief:** Erleichterung.
9 **turnip:** (weiße) Rübe.
12 **wanting:** *wanted.*
14 **broken harvest:** Mißernte.
16 **furtively** (adv.): heimlich, verstohlen.
17 **larceny:** Diebstahl.
18 **dolefully** (adv.): traurig, mißmutig.
20 **There's a queer lad!:** Du bist ein komischer Junge!
  to be slapped: Schläge bekommen.

school, young fellow, that you don't know the name
of your deed?

CHRISTY *(bashfully)*. I'm slow at learning, a middling
scholar only.

5 MICHAEL. If you're a dunce itself, you'd have a right to
know that larceny's robbing and stealing. Is it for the
like of that you're wanting?

CHRISTY *(with a flash of family pride)*. And I the son of
a strong farmer *(with a sudden qualm)*, God rest his
10 soul, could have bought up the whole of your old
house a while since from the butt of his tail-pocket
and not have missed the weight of it gone.

MICHAEL *(impressed)*. If it's not stealing, it's maybe
something big.

15 CHRISTY *(flattered)*. Aye; it's maybe something big.

JIMMY. He's a wicked-looking young fellow. Maybe he
followed after a young woman on a lonesome night.

CHRISTY *(shocked)*. Oh, the saints forbid, mister. I was
all times a decent lad.

20 PHILLY *(turning on Jimmy)*. You're a silly man, Jimmy
Farrell. He said his father was a farmer a while since,
and there's himself now in a poor state. Maybe the
land was grabbed from him, and he did what any
decent man would do.

---

3 **bashfully** (adv.): verschämt, schüchtern.
3f. **a middling scholar only:** nur ein mäßiger (leidlicher) Schüler.
5 **dunce:** Dummkopf, Esel.
8 **flash:** Blitzstrahl; hier: (fig.) Aufflammen, Anflug.
9 **strong farmer:** ,dicker' Bauer.
 qualm: ungutes Gefühl, Gewissensbiß.
11 **from the butt of his tail-pocket:** aus dem Untersten seiner Rock-
 schoßtasche (*butt:* Stamm, Stiel, Ende).
15 **aye** (dial.): ja!
23 **to grab:** entreißen.

MICHAEL *(to Christy, mysteriously)*. Was it bailiffs?

CHRISTY. The divil a one.

MICHAEL. Agents?

CHRISTY. The divil a one.

5 MICHAEL. Landlords?

CHRISTY *(peevishly)*. Ah, not at all, I'm saying. You'd
see the like of them stories on any little paper of a
Munster town. But I'm not calling to mind any person, gentle, simple, judge or jury, did the like of me.

10 *(They all draw nearer with delighted curiosity.)*

PHILLY. Well that lad's a puzzle-the-world.

JIMMY. He'd beat Dan Davies' Circus or the holy mis-
sioners making sermons on the villainy of man. Try
him again, Philly.

15 PHILLY. Did you strike golden guineas out of solder,
young fellow, or shilling coins itself?

CHRISTY. I did not, mister, not sixpence nor a farthing
coin.

JIMMY. Did you marry three wives maybe? I'm told
20 there's a sprinkling have done that among the holy
Luthers of the preaching North.

---

1 **bailiff:** Vollstreckungsbeamter.
2 **the divil a one:** der Teufel noch mal!
3 **agent:** Verwalter.
5 **landlord:** Landeigentümer, Gutsbesitzer.
6 **peevishly** (adv.): verdrießlich.
11 **puzzle-the-world:** Welträtsel.
12 **to beat:** schlagen, übertreffen.
12 f. **missioner:** *missionary*.
13 **villainy:** Schurkerei, Schandtaten.
15 **guinea:** Goldmünze im Wert von 21 Schilling.
   solder: Lötmetall.
17 **farthing:** ¼ Penny; (fig.) Heller.
20 **a sprinkling have done that:** wenige einzelne, Verstreute haben das
   getan.

CHRISTY *(shyly)*. I never married with one, let alone with
a couple or three.

PHILLY. Maybe he went fighting for the Boers, the like
of the man beyond, was judged to be hanged, quartered, and drawn. Were you off east, young fellow,
fighting bloody wars for Kruger and the freedom of
the Boers?

CHRISTY. I never left my own parish till Tuesday was a
week.

PEGEEN *(coming from counter)*. He's done nothing, so.
(To Christy.) If you didn't commit murder or a bad
nasty thing, or false coining, or robbery, or butchery
or the like of them, there isn't anything would be
worth your troubling for to run from now. You did
nothing at all.

CHRISTY *(his feelings hurt)*. That's an unkindly thing to
be saying to a poor orphaned traveller, has a prison
behind him, and hanging before, and hell's gap gaping below.

---

3 **Boer:** Bure (Nachkommen der niederländischen und deutschen
Ansiedler in Südafrika).

4f. **to be hanged, quartered, and drawn:** Anspielung auf die alte
Hinrichtungsprozedur für Hochverrat, bei der der Verurteilte zum
Richtplatz gezogen, d. h. gekarrt, dann gehängt und gevierteilt
wurde.

6 **Kruger:** Oom Paulus K. (1825–1904), südafrikanischer Staatsmann,
der den Eintritt der Südafrikanischen Republik in den Burenkrieg
(1899–1902) gegen die Errichtung eines geschlossenen britischen
Kolonialreichs nicht verhindern konnte.

8f. **till Tuesday was a week:** seit Dienstag vor einer Woche.

12 **nasty:** widerlich, ekelhaft.
false coining: Falschmünzerei.

17 **orphaned:** verwaist.

18 **hell's gap:** Höllenspalte, -schlund.

18f. **to gape:** gähnen, sich auftun.

PEGEEN (*with a sign to the men to be quiet*). You're only
saying it. You did nothing at all. A soft lad the like of
you wouldn't slit the wind-pipe of a screeching sow.

CHRISTY (*offended*). You're not speaking the truth.

5 PEGEEN (*in mock rage*). Not speaking the truth, is it?
Would you have me knock the head of you with the
butt of the broom?

CHRISTY (*twisting round on her with a sharp cry of
horror*). Don't strike me. . . . I killed my poor father,

10 Tuesday was a week, for doing the like of that.

PEGEEN (*with blank amazement*). Is it killed your father?

CHRISTY (*subsiding*). With the help of God I did surely,
and that the Holy Immaculate Mother may intercede
for his soul.

15 PHILLY (*retreating with Jimmy*). There's a daring fellow.

JIMMY. Oh, glory be to God!

MICHAEL (*with great respect*). That was a hanging crime,
mister honey. You should have had good reason for
doing the like of that.

20 CHRISTY (*in a very reasonable tone*). He was a dirty man,
God forgive him, and he getting old and crusty, the
way I couldn't put up with him at all.

---

3 **to slit:** (auf)schlitzen, aufschneiden.
  wind-pipe: Luftröhre, Gurgel.
  to screech: schreien, kreischen, quieken.
  sow: Sau.
5 **in mock rage:** in gespieltem Zorn.
11 **with blank amazement:** mit blankem, d. h. offensichtlichem Entsetzen.
12 **to subside:** nachlassen, leiser werden.
13 **immaculate:** unbefleckt.
  to intercede: sich verwenden, Fürsprache einlegen.
15 **There's a daring fellow:** So ein Teufelskerl!
21 **crusty:** mürrisch, reizbar.
22 **to put up with:** sich gefallen lassen, hinnehmen.

PEGEEN. And you shot him dead?

CHRISTY *(shaking his head)*. I never used weapons. I've no licence, and I'm a law-fearing man.

MICHAEL. It was with a hilted knife maybe? I'm told, in
5 the big world, it's bloody knives they use.

CHRISTY *(loudly, scandalized)*. Do you take me for a slaughter-boy?

PEGEEN. You never hanged him, the way Jimmy Farrell hanged his dog from the licence and had it screeching
10 and wriggling three hours at the butt of a string, and himself swearing it was a dead dog, and the peelers swearing it had life?

CHRISTY. I did not then. I just riz the loy and let fall the edge of it on the ridge of his skull, and he went down
15 at my feet like an empty sack, and never let a grunt or groan from him at all.

MICHAEL *(making a sign to Pegeen to fill Christy's glass)*. And what way weren't you hanged, mister? Did you bury him then?

20 CHRISTY *(considering)*. Aye. I buried him then. Wasn't I digging spuds in the field?

MICHAEL. And the peelers never followed after you the eleven days that you're out?

---

3 **licence:** Abk. für *gun licence:* Waffenschein.
  law-fearing: die Gesetze fürchtend, friedlich.
4 **hilted:** mit einem Griff versehen.
7 **slaughter-boy:** Metzgerjunge.
9 **from the licence:** hier: wegen der Hundesteuer.
10 **to wriggle:** sich winden, zappeln.
13 **riz** (dial.): *raised*.
  loy (ir.): langer, schmaler Spaten.
14 **ridge:** Kamm(linie).
15 **grunt:** Grunzen.
21 **to dig spuds:** Kartoffeln ausmachen.

CHRISTY *(shaking his head)*. Never a one of them and I
walking forward facing hog, dog, or divil on the
highway of the road.

PHILLY *(nodding wisely)*. It's only with a common week-
day kind of a murderer them lads would be trusting
their carcase, and that man should be a great terror
when his temper's roused.

MICHAEL. He should then. *(To Christy.)* And where was
it, mister honey, that you did the deed?

CHRISTY *(looking at him with suspicion)*. Oh, a distant
place, master of the house, a windy corner of high
distant hills.

PHILLY *(nodding with approval)*. He's a close man and
he's right surely.

PEGEEN. That'd be a lad with the sense of Solomon to
have for a pot-boy, Michael James, if it's the truth
you're seeking one at all.

PHILLY. The peelers is fearing him, and if you'd that lad
in the house there isn't one of them would come
smelling around if the dogs itself were lapping poteen
from the dung-pit of the yard.

JIMMY. Bravery's a treasure in a lonesome place, and a
lad would kill his father, I'm thinking, would face a
foxy divil with a pitchpike on the flags of hell.

---

  2 **hog:** Schwein.
  4 **to nod:** mit dem Kopf nicken.
  6 **carcase** (= *carcass*): Leichnam.
 13 **close:** zurückhaltend, verschwiegen.
 20 **to lap:** auflecken.
    poteen (ir.): aus einer Schwarzbrennerei stammender Whisky.
 21 **dung-pit:** Mistgrube, Misthaufen.
 22 **bravery:** Tapferkeit, Unerschrockenheit.
 24 **foxy:** schlau.
    pitchpike: Heu-, Mistgabel.

PEGEEN. It's the truth they're saying, and if I'd that lad in the house, I wouldn't be fearing the loosèd khaki cut-throats, or the walking dead.

CHRISTY *(swelling with surprise and triumph)*. Well, glory be to God!

MICHAEL *(with deference)*. Would you think well to stop here and be pot-boy, mister honey, if we gave you good wages, and didn't destroy you with the weight of work?

SHAWN *(coming forward uneasily)*. That'd be a queer kind to bring into a decent quiet household with the like of Pegeen Mike.

PEGEEN *(very sharply)*. Will you whisht. Who's speaking to you?

SHAWN *(retreating)*. A bloody-handed murderer the like of. . . .

PEGEEN *(snapping at him)*. Whisht, I'm saying, we'll take no fooling from your like at all. *(To Christy with a honeyed voice.)* And you, young fellow, you'd have a right to stop I'm thinking, for we'd do our all and utmost to content your needs.

CHRISTY *(overcome with wonder)*. And I'd be safe this place from the searching law?

MICHAEL. You would surely. If they're not fearing you itself, the peelers in this place is decent, droughty

---

2f. **the loosèd khaki cut-throats:** die losgelassenen khakifarbenen Halsabschneider, d. h. Soldaten.
3 **walking dead:** wandernder Toter, Wiedergänger.
6 **deference:** Achtung, Ehrerbietung.
8 **to destroy:** umbringen.
17 **to snap at s.o.:** jdn. anfahren, jdm. bissig antworten.
25 **droughty:** durstig.

poor fellows, wouldn't touch a cur dog and not give
warning in the dead of night.

PEGEEN *(very kindly and persuasively)*. Let you stop a
short while anyhow. Aren't you destroyed walking
with your feet in bleeding blisters, and your whole
skin needing washing like a Wicklow sheep.

CHRISTY *(looking round with satisfaction)*. It's a nice
room, and if it's not humbugging me you are, I'm
thinking that I'll surely stay.

JIMMY *(jumps up)*. Now, by the grace of God, herself
will be safe this night, with a man killed his father
holding danger from the door, and let you come on,
Michael James, or they'll have the best stuff drunk at
the wake.

MICHAEL *(going to the door with Men)*. And begging
your pardon, mister, what name will we call you for
we'd like to know.

CHRISTY. Christopher Mahon.

MICHAEL. Well, God bless you Christy, and a good rest
till we meet again when the sun'll be rising to the
noon of day.

CHRISTY. God bless you all.

MEN. God bless you. *(They go out except Shawn who
lingers at door.)*

SHAWN *(to Pegeen)*. Are you wanting me to stop along
with you and keep you from harm?

---

1 **cur dog:** Wachhund.
1 f. **to give warning:** Alarm schlagen.
2 **in the dead of the night:** in der Stille der Nacht.
3 **persuasively** (adv.): überredend.
5 **blister:** Blase.
8 **to humbug:** beschwindeln, betrügen.

PEGEEN. *(gruffly)*. Didn't you say you were fearing
Father Reilly?

SHAWN. There'd be no harm staying now, I'm thinking,
and himself in it too.

5 PEGEEN. You wouldn't stay when there was need for
you, and let you step off nimble this time when
there's none.

SHAWN. Didn't I say it was Father Reilly. . . .

PEGEEN. Go on then to Father Reilly *(in a jeering tone)*,
10   and let him put you in the holy brotherhoods and
leave that lad to me.

SHAWN. If I meet the Widow Quin. . . .

PEGEEN. Go on, I'm saying, and don't be waking this
place with your noise. *(She hustles him out and bolts*
15   *door.)* That lad would wear the spirits from the saints
of peace. *(Bustles about, then takes off her apron and*
pins it up in the window as a blind, Christy watching
her timidly. Then she comes to him and speaks with
bland good humour.) Let you stretch out now by the
20   fire, young fellow. You should be destroyed travelling.

CHRISTY *(shyly again, drawing off his boots)*. I'm tired
surely, walking wild eleven days and waking fearful in

---

1 **gruffly:** ruppig, mürrisch.
6 **nimble:** hier: *nimbly* (adv.): flink.
9 **in a jeering tone:** in höhnischem Ton *(to jeer:* spotten, höhnen).
10 **brotherhood:** Bruderschaft; Kloster.
14 **to hustle s.o. out:** jdn. hinausdrängen.
　　to bolt: verriegeln.
15 **to wear the spirits:** zermürben.
16 **to bustle about:** herumhantieren.
17 **blind:** Vorhang, Blende.
19 **bland:** sanft, einschmeichelnd.

the night. *(He holds up one of his feet, feeling his blisters and looking at it with compassion.)*

PEGEEN *(standing beside him, watching him with delight)*. You should have had great people in your family, I'm thinking, with the little small feet you have, and you with a kind of a quality name, the like of what you'd find on the great powers and potentates of France and Spain.

CHRISTY *(with pride)*. We were great surely, with wide and windy acres of rich Munster land.

PEGEEN. Wasn't I telling you, and you a fine, handsome young fellow with a noble brow.

CHRISTY *(with a flash of delighted surprise)*. Is it me?

PEGEEN. Aye. Did you never hear that from the young girls where you come from in the west or south?

CHRISTY *(with venom)*. I did not then. . . . Oh, they're bloody liars in the naked parish where I grew a man.

PEGEEN. If they are itself, you've heard it these days, I'm thinking, and you walking the world telling out your story to young girls or old.

CHRISTY. I've told my story no place till this night, Pegeen Mike, and it's foolish I was here, maybe, to be talking free, but you're decent people, I'm think-

---

2 **compassion:** Mitleid.
6 **a quality name:** Anspielung auf den französischen Marschall Comte de Mac-Mahon (1808–93), der 1873 Präsident der Dritten Republik wurde und 1879 zurücktrat.
7 **potentate:** Machthaber.
12 **brow:** Stirn, Antlitz.
13 **Is it me?:** Meinen Sie mich?
16 **with venom:** giftig.
17 **liar:** Lügner(in).
18 **If they are itself, you've heard it:** selbst wenn sie das sind, so hast du es doch gehört.

ing, and yourself a kindly woman, the way I wasn't
fearing you at all.

PEGEEN *(filling a sack with straw, right)*. You've said the
like of that, maybe, in every cot and cabin where
5   you've met a young girl on your way.

CHRISTY *(going over to her, gradually raising his voice)*.
I've said it nowhere till this night, I'm telling you, for
I've seen none the like of you the eleven days I am
walking the world, looking over a low ditch or a high
10   ditch on my north or south, into stony scattered
fields, or scribes of bog, where you'd see young
limber girls, and fine prancing women making laugh-
ter with the men.

PEGEEN *(nodding with approval)*. If you weren't de-
15   stroyed travelling you'd have as much talk and streeleen, I'm thinking, as Owen Roe O'Sullivan or the
poets of the Dingle Bay, and I've heard all times it's
the poets are your like, fine fiery fellows with great
rages when their temper's roused.

20   CHRISTY *(drawing a little nearer to her)*. You've a power
of rings, God bless you, and would there be any
offence if I was asking are you single now?

PEGEEN. What would I want wedding so young?

CHRISTY *(with relief)*. We're alike, so.

25   PEGEEN *(putting sack on settle and beating it up)*. I never

---

4 **cot:** Kate, Hütte.
11 **scribes of bog:** langgezogene Moorstreifen, in denen Torf gestochen
   wird.
12 **limber:** biegsam, geschmeidig.
   to prance: einherstolzieren.
15 f. **streeleen** (ir.): Wortgeplätscher, Geplauder.
20 f. **a power of rings:** eine Riesenmenge, Unmenge an Ringen, mäch-
   tig viel Ringe.

killed my father. I'd be afeard to do that, except I was
the like of yourself with blind rages tearing me
within, for I'm thinking you should have had great
tussling when the end was come.

CHRISTY *(expanding with delight at the first confidential
talk he has ever had with a woman)*. We had not then.
It was a hard woman was come over the hill, and if he
was always a crusty kind, when he'd a hard woman
setting him on, not the divil himself or his four fathers
could put up with him at all.

PEGEEN *(with curiosity)*. And isn't it a great wonder that
one wasn't fearing you?

CHRISTY *(very confidentially)*. Up to the day I killed my
father, there wasn't a person in Ireland knew the kind
I was, and I there drinking, waking, eating, sleeping,
a quiet, simple poor fellow with no man giving me
heed.

PEGEEN *(getting a quilt out of cupboard and putting it on
the sack)*. It was the girls were giving you heed
maybe, and I'm thinking it's most conceit you'd have
to be gaming with their like.

CHRISTY *(shaking his head, with simplicity)*. Not the girls
itself, and I won't tell you a lie. There wasn't anyone
heeding me in that place saving only the dumb beasts
of the field. *(He sits down at fire.)*

PEGEEN *(with disappointment)*. And I thinking you
should have been living the like of a king of Norway

---

4 **tussling:** hartes Ringen.
9 **to set s.o. on:** jdn. aufhetzen.
16f. **to give s.o. heed:** jdn. beachten (*heed:* Aufmerksamkeit).
18 **quilt:** Stepp-, Bettdecke.
24 **to heed:** beachten.

or the Eastern world. *(She comes and sits beside him after placing bread and mug of milk on the table.)*

CHRISTY *(laughing piteously).* The like of a king, is it! And I after toiling, moiling, digging, dodging from
5 the dawn till dusk with never a sight of joy or sport saving only when I'd be abroad in the dark night poaching rabbits on hills, for I was a divil to poach, God forgive me *(very naïvely)*, and I near got six months for going with a dung-fork and stabbing a
10 fish.

PEGEEN. And it's that you'd call sport is it, to be abroad in the darkness with yourself alone?

CHRISTY. I did, God help me, and there I'd be as happy as the sunshine of St. Martin's Day, watching the
15 light passing the north or the patches of fog, till I'd hear a rabbit starting to screech and I'd go running in the furze. Then when I'd my full share I'd come walking down where you'd see the ducks and geese stretched sleeping on the highway of the road,
20 and before I'd pass the dunghill, I'd hear himself snoring out, a loud lonesome snore he'd be making all times, the while he was sleeping, and he a man'd be raging all times the while he was waking, like a

---

2 **mug:** Krug, Becher.
3 **piteously** (adv.): mitleidig; kläglich.
4 **to toil:** schuften.
   to moil: sich placken, abquälen.
   to dodge (dial.): sich winden und wenden.
4 f. **from the dawn till dusk:** von der Morgen- bis zur Abenddämmerung.
7 **to poach:** wildern.
9 **to stab:** (er)stechen, durchbohren.
15 **patches of fog:** Nebelfelder, -flächen.
21 **to snore:** schnarchen.

gaudy officer you'd hear cursing and damning and swearing oaths.

PEGEEN. Providence and Mercy, spare us all!

CHRISTY. It's that you'd say surely if you seen him and he after drinking for weeks, rising up in the red dawn, or before it maybe, and going out into the yard as naked as an ash tree in the moon of May, and shying clods again the visage of the stars till he'd put the fear of death into the banbhs and the screeching sows.

PEGEEN. I'd be well-nigh afeard of that lad myself, I'm thinking. And there was no one in it but the two of you alone?

CHRISTY. The divil a one, though he'd sons and daughters walking all great states and territories of the world, and not a one of them to this day would say their seven curses on him, and they rousing up to let a cough or sneeze, maybe, in the deadness of the night.

PEGEEN (*nodding her head*). Well, you should have been a queer lot. . . . I never cursed my father the like of that though I'm twenty and more years of age.

CHRISTY. Then you'd have cursed mine, I'm telling you,

---

1 **gaudy:** herausgeputzt.
2 **oath:** Eid.
3 **providence:** Vorsehung.
7 **ash tree:** Esche.
  in the moon of May: im Maienmond, im Monat Mai.
  to shy: werfen, schleudern.
  clod: (Erd-)Klumpen, Scholle.
8 **again:** against.
9 **banbhs** (ir., pl.): Ferkel.
10 **well-nigh** (adv.): fast.
  that lad: hier etwa: der alte Knabe.
16f. **to rouse up to let a cough or sneeze:** aufwachen, um zu husten oder niesen.
17 **in the deadness of the night:** *in the dead of the night.*

and he a man never gave peace to any saving when
he'd get two months or three, or be locked in the
asylum for battering peelers or assaulting men *(with
depression)*, the way it was a bitter life he led me till I
5 did up a Tuesday and halve his skull.

PEGEEN *(putting her hand on his shoulder)*. Well, you'll
have peace in this place, Christy Mahon, and none to
trouble you, and it's near time a fine lad the like of
you should have your good share of the earth.

10 CHRISTY. It's time surely, and I a seemly fellow with
great strength in me and bravery of. . . . *(Some one
knocks.)*

CHRISTY *(clinging to Pegeen)*. Oh, glory! it's late for
knocking, and this last while I'm in terror of the
15 peelers, and the walking dead. . . . *(Knocking again.)*

PEGEEN. Who's there?

VOICE *(outside)*. Me.

PEGEEN. Who's me?

VOICE. The Widow Quin.

20 PEGEEN *(jumping up and giving him the bread and milk)*.
Go on now with your supper, and let on to be sleepy,
for if she found you were such a warrant to talk, she'd
be stringing gabble till the dawn of day.

*(Christy takes bread and sits shyly with his back to the
25 door.)*

---

3 **asylum:** Irrenanstalt.
   to batter: prügeln, übel zurichten.
   to assault: tätlich angreifen.
5 **to do up:** (fig.) sich erheben, aufbegehren.
   to halve: halbieren.
10 **seemly:** hier: ansehnlich.
13 **to cling to s.o.:** sich an jdn. klammern.
21 **let on to be sleepy:** stell dich schläfrig.
23 **to string gabble:** endlos schnattern (*to string:* aufreihen).

PEGEEN *(opening door, with temper)*. What ails you, or what is it you're wanting at this hour of the night?

WIDOW QUIN *(coming in a step and peering at Christy)*. I'm after meeting Shawn Keogh and Father Reilly below, who told me of your curiosity man, and they fearing by this time he was maybe roaring, romping on your hands with drink.

PEGEEN *(pointing to Christy)*. Look now, is he roaring, and he stretched out drowsy with his supper, and his mug of milk. Walk down and tell that to Father Reilly and to Shaneen Keogh.

WIDOW QUIN *(coming forward)*. I'll not see them again, for I've their word to lead that lad forward for to lodge with me.

PEGEEN *(in blank amazement)*. This night, is it?

WIDOW QUIN *(going over)*. This night. "It isn't fitting," says the priesteen, "to have his likeness lodging with an orphaned girl." *(To Christy.)* God save you, mister!

CHRISTY *(shyly)*. God save you kindly.

WIDOW QUIN *(looking at him with half-amused curiosity)*. Well, aren't you a little smiling fellow? It should have been great and bitter torments did rouse your spirits to a deed of blood.

---

1 **with temper:** in Wut, gereizt.
3 **to peer at:** (genau) begucken.
5 **your curiosity man:** dein Wunderknabe.
6 **to romp:** toben.
7 **on s.o.'s hands:** jdm. zur Last.
9 **drowsy:** schläfrig, träge.
17 **priesteen:** Diminutiv von *priest*.
   to have his likeness lodging with s.o.: so einen bei jdm. wohnen zu lassen.
24 **deed of blood:** Bluttat.

CHRISTY *(doubtfully)*. It should, maybe.

WIDOW QUIN. It's more than "maybe" I'm saying, and
it'd soften my heart to see you sitting so simple with
your cup and cake, and you fitter to be saying your
5   catechism than slaying your da.

PEGEEN *(at counter, washing glasses)*. There's talking
when any'd see he's fit to be holding his head high
with the wonders of the world. Walk on from this, for
I'll not have him tormented and he destroyed travel-
10   ling since Tuesday was a week.

WIDOW QUIN *(peaceably)*. We'll be walking surely when
his supper's done, and you'll find we're great company, young fellow, when it's of the like of you and
me you'd hear the penny poets singing in an August
15   Fair.

CHRISTY *(innocently)*. Did you kill your father?

PEGEEN *(contemptuously)*. She did not. She hit himself
with a worn pick, and the rusted poison did corrode
his blood the way he never overed it and died after.
20   That was a sneaky kind of murder did win small glory
with the boys itself. *(She crosses to Christy's left.)*

WIDOW QUIN *(with good-humour)*. If it didn't, maybe all
knows a widow woman has buried her children and

---

5 **to slay:** erschlagen.
8 **the wonders of the world:** die Weltwunder.
    walk on from this: mach, daß Du weiterkommst!
11 **peaceably** (adv.): friedfertig.
14 **penny poet:** Bänkelsänger.
17 **contemptuously** (adv.): verächtlich.
17 f. **She hit himself with a worn pick:** sie schlug ihn mit einer abgenutz-
    ten Hacke.
18 f. **the rusted poison did corrode his blood:** das rostige Gift zerfraß
    sein Blut.
19 **he never overed it:** er hat es nie überwunden, sich nie davon erholt.
20 **sneaky:** hinterhältig, gemein.

destroyed her man is a wiser comrade for a young lad
than a girl the like of you who'd go helter-skeltering
after any man would let you a wink upon the road.

PEGEEN *(breaking out into wild rage).* And you'll say
that, Widow Quin, and you gasping with the rage you
had racing the hill beyond to look on his face.

WIDOW QUIN *(laughing derisively).* Me, is it! Well,
Father Reilly has cuteness to divide you now. *(She
pulls Christy up.)* There's great temptation in a man
did slay his da, and we'd best be going, young fellow;
so rise up and come with me.

PEGEEN *(seizing his arm).* He'll not stir. He's pot-boy in
this place and I'll not have him stolen off and kidnab-
bed while himself's abroad.

WIDOW QUIN. It'd be a crazy pot-boy'd lodge him in the
shebeen where he works by day, so you'd have a right
to come on, young fellow, till you see my little
houseen, a perch off on the rising hill.

PEGEEN. Wait till morning, Christy Mahon, wait till you
lay eyes on her leaky thatch is growing more pasture

2f. **to go helter-skeltering after s.o.:** jdm. holterdiepolter nachrennen.
5 **to gasp:** keuchen, schnaufen.
7 **derisively** (adv.): spöttisch, höhnisch.
8 **cuteness:** Scharfsinn, Verstand.
12 **to stir:** sich rühren, bewegen.
13f. **to kidnab** (= *kidnap*): (Kinder) rauben, entführen.
14 **while himself's abroad:** während er (d. h. Pegeens Vater) außer Hauses ist.
15f. **It'd be a crazy pot-boy'd lodge ... by day:** nur ein närrischer Schankbursche würde sich in der Kneipe einquartieren, wo er tagsüber arbeitet.
18 **houseen:** Häuschen.
    a perch off: eine Rute (Längenmaß) entfernt.
20 **leaky:** leck, wasserdurchlässig.
    thatch: Strohdach.

for her buck goat than her square of fields, and she
without a tramp itself to keep in order her place at all.

WIDOW QUIN. When you see me contriving in my little
gardens, Christy Mahon, you'll swear the Lord God
5   formed me to be living lone and that there isn't my
match in Mayo for thatching or mowing or shearing a
sheep.

PEGEEN *(with noisy scorn)*. It's true the Lord God
formed you to contrive indeed! Doesn't the world
10   know you reared a black ram at your own breast, so
that the Lord Bishop of Connaught felt the elements
of a Christian, and he eating it after in a kidney stew?
Doesn't the world know you've been seen shaving the
foxy skipper from France for a threepenny bit and a
15   sop of grass tobacco would wring the liver from a
mountain goat you'd meet lepping the hills?

WIDOW QUIN *(with amusement)*. Do you hear her now,
young fellow? Do you hear the way she'll be rating at
your own self when a week is by?

---

1 **buck goat:** Ziegenbock.
2 **tramp:** Wanderbursche, Landstreicher.
3 **to contrive:** hantieren, planen; Ränke schmieden (vgl. Z. 9).
5 f. **there isn't my match:** es gibt nicht meinesgleichen.
6 **to thatch:** mit Stroh decken.
   to shear: scheren.
10 **to rear:** ernähren, großziehen.
    ram: Widder.
11 f. **the Lord Bishop of Connaught felt ... in a kidney stew:** der
    hochwürdige Bischof merkte Spuren von was Christlichem, als er
    ihn (d. h. den Widder) später in einem Niereneintopf gegessen hat.
14 **skipper:** Schiffer, Kapitän.
    threepenny bit: Dreipfennig-Bissen.
15 **sop of grass tobacco:** Büschel ungetrockneter Tabakblätter.
16 **to lep** (ir.): *to leap*.
18 **to rate at s.o.:** jdn. ausschelten.

PEGEEN *(to Christy)*. Don't heed her. Tell her to go on
  into her pigsty and not plague us here.

WIDOW QUIN. I'm going; but he'll come with me.

PEGEEN *(shaking him)*. Are you dumb, young fellow?

CHRISTY *(timidly to Widow Quin)*. God increase you; but
  I'm pot-boy in this place, and it's here I'd liefer stay.

PEGEEN *(triumphantly)*. Now you've heard him, and go
  on from this.

WIDOW QUIN *(looking round the room)*. It's lonesome
  this hour crossing the hill, and if he won't come along
  with me, I'd have a right maybe to stop this night with
  yourselves. Let me stretch out on the settle, Pegeen
  Mike, and himself can lie by the hearth.

PEGEEN *(short and fiercely)*. Faith I won't. Quit off or I
  will send you now.

WIDOW QUIN *(gathering her shawl up)*. Well, it's a terror
  to be aged a score! *(To Christy.)* God bless you now,
  young fellow, and let you be wary, or there's right
  torment will await you here if you go romancing with
  her like, and she waiting only, as they bade me say,
  on a sheep-skin parchment to be wed with Shawn
  Keogh of Killakeen. *(She goes out.)*

CHRISTY *(going to Pegeen, as she bolts door)*. What's that
  she's after saying?

---

 2 **pigsty:** Schweinestall.
   to plague: ärgern, belästigen.
 5 **God increase you:** etwa: Gott mehre Euer Gut *(to increase:* ver-
   mehren).
 6 **liefer** (dial.): lieber.
14 **fiercely** (adv.): heftig, grimmig.
18 **let you be wary:** sieh dich vor!
19 f. **to go romancing with her like:** mit so einer anbändeln (wie der
   Held in einem Liebesroman).
21 **sheep-skin parchment:** Pergament aus Schafshaut.

PEGEEN. Lies and blather, you've no call to mind. Well
    isn't Shawn Keogh an impudent fellow to send up
    spying on me? Wait till I lay hands on him. Let him
    wait, I'm saying.
5 CHRISTY. And you're not wedding him at all?
PEGEEN. I wouldn't wed him if a bishop came walking for
    to join us here.
CHRISTY. That God in glory may be thanked for that.
PEGEEN. There's your bed now. I've put a quilt upon you
10   I'm after quilting a while since with my own two
    hands, and you'd best stretch out now for your sleep,
    and may God give you a good rest till I call you in the
    morning when the cocks will crow.
CHRISTY *(as she goes to inner room)*. May God and Mary
15   and St. Patrick bless you and reward you for your
    kindly talk. *(She shuts the door behind her. He settles
    his bed slowly, feeling the quilt with immense satisfac-
    tion.)* Well it's a clean bed and soft with it, and it's
    great luck and company I've won me in the end of
20   time – two fine women fighting for the likes of me –,
    till I'm thinking this night wasn't I a foolish fellow not
    to kill my father in the years gone by.

CURTAIN

---

1 **blather** (= *blether*): unsinniges Geschwätz.
2 **impudent:** unverschämt, schamlos.
10 **to quilt:** steppen, durchnähen; füttern, polstern.

Act II

Scene as before. Brilliant morning light. Christy, looking bright and cheerful, is cleaning a girl's boot.

CHRISTY *(to himself, counting jugs on dresser).* Half a
hundred beyond. Ten there. A score that's above.
Eighty jugs. Six cups and a broken one. Two plates.
A power of glasses. Bottles, a school-master'd be
hard set to count, and enough in them, I'm thinking,
to drunken all the wealth and wisdom of the County
Clare. *(He puts down the boot carefully.)* There's her
boots now, nice and decent for her evening use, and
isn't it grand brushes she has? *(He puts them down
and goes by degrees to the looking-glass.)* Well, this'd
be a fine place to be my whole life talking out with
swearing Christians in place of my old dogs and cat,
and I stalking around, smoking my pipe and drinking
my fill, and never a day's work but drawing a cork an
odd time, or wiping a glass, or rinsing out a shiny
tumbler for a decent man. *(He takes the looking-glass
from the wall and puts it on the back of a chair; then*

---

9 **to drunken** (dial.): ertränken.
12 **grand:** großartig, prächtig.
14 **to talk out:** sich aussprechen.
16 **to stalk around:** stolzieren.
16f. **to drink one's fill:** sich satt trinken.
18 **to rinse out:** (aus)spülen.
19 **tumbler:** fuß- und henkelloses Trinkglas.

sits down in front of it and begins washing his face.)
Didn't I know rightly I was handsome, though it was
the divil's own mirror we had beyond, would twist a
squint across an angel's brow, and I'll be growing fine
5 from this day, the way I'll have a soft lovely skin on
me and won't be the like of the clumsy young fellows
do be ploughing all times in the earth and dung. *(He
starts.)* Is she coming again? *(He looks out.)* Stranger
girls. God help me, where'll I hide myself away and
10 my long neck naked to the world. *(He looks out.)* I'd
best go to the room maybe till I'm dressed again.
*(He gathers up his coat and the looking-glass, and
runs into the inner room. The door is pushed open,
and Susan Brady looks in, and knocks on door.)*
15 SUSAN. There's nobody in it. *(Knocks again.)*
NELLY *(pushing her in and following her, with Honor
Blake and Sara Tansey).* It'd be early for them both
to be out walking the hill.
SUSAN. I'm thinking Shawn Keogh was making game of
20 us and there's no such man in it at all.
HONOR *(pointing to straw and quilt).* Look at that. He's
been sleeping there in the night. Well, it'll be a hard
case if he's gone off now, the way we'll never set our
eyes on a man killed his father, and we after rising
25 early and destroying ourselves running fast on the
hill.
NELLY. Are you thinking them's his boots?
SARA *(taking them up).* If they are, there should be his

---

3 **to twist:** hier: verdrehen, verzerren.
6 **clumsy:** unbeholfen, plump.
7 **to plough:** pflügen.
22 f. **a hard case:** ein hoffnungsloser Fall.

father's track on them. Did you never read in the
papers the way murdered men do bleed and drip?

SUSAN. Is that blood there, Sara Tansey?

SARA *(smelling it)*. That's bog water, I'm thinking, but
it's his own they are surely, for I never seen the like of
them for whity mud, and red mud, and turf on them,
and the fine sands of the sea. That man's been
walking, I'm telling you. *(She goes down right, putting on one of his boots.)*

SUSAN *(going to window)*. Maybe he's stolen off to
Belmullet with the boots of Michael James, and you'd
have a right so to follow after him, Sara Tansey, and
you the one yoked the ass cart and drove ten miles to
set your eyes on the man bit the yellow lady's nostril
on the northern shore. *(She looks out.)*

SARA *(running to window, with one boot on)*. Don't be
talking, and we fooled to-day. *(Putting on other
boot.)* There's a pair do fit me well, and I'll be
keeping them for walking to the priest, when you'd
be ashamed this place, going up winter and summer
with nothing worth while to confess at all.

HONOR *(who has been listening at inner door)*. Whisht!
there's some one inside the room. *(She pushes door a
chink open.)* It's a man.

*(Sara kicks off boots and puts them where they were.
They all stand in a line looking through chink.)*

---

1 **track:** Spur.
2 **to drip:** tropfen.
13 **to yoke:** anspannen, -schirren.
14 **nostril:** Nasenloch, Nüster.
21 **to confess:** beichten.
25 **to kick off:** abwerfen.

SARA. I'll call him. Mister! Mister! *(He puts in his head.)*
Is Pegeen within?

CHRISTY *(coming in as meek as a mouse, with the looking-glass held behind his back.)* She's above on the
5   cnuceen, seeking the nanny goats, the way she'd have
a sup of goat's milk for to colour my tea.

SARA. And asking your pardon, is it you's the man killed
his father?

CHRISTY *(sidling toward the nail where the glass was
10   hanging).* I am, God help me!

SARA *(taking eggs she has brought).* Then my thousand
welcomes to you, and I've run up with a brace of
duck's eggs for your food to-day. Pegeen's ducks is no
use, but these are the real rich sort. Hold out your
15   hand and you'll see it's no lie I'm telling you.

CHRISTY *(coming forward shyly, and holding out his left
hand).* They're a great and weighty size.

SUSAN. And I run up with a pat of butter, for it'd be a
poor thing to have you eating your spuds dry, and you
20   after running a great way since you did destroy your
da.

CHRISTY. Thank you kindly.

HONOR. And I brought you a little cut of a cake, for you
should have a thin stomach on you and you that
25   length walking the world.

---

3 **meek:** sanft, demütig.
5 **cnuceen** (ir.): Hügel(chen).
   nanny goat: Ziege.
6 **sup:** kleine Menge, kleiner Schluck.
9 **to sidle towards s.th.:** sich seitwärts auf etwas zubewegen.
12 **a brace of . . .:** ein Paar . . .
18 **pat:** Stück, Schlag.
23 **cut:** Stück.
24 **to have a thin stomach on o.s.:** einen hängenden Magen haben.

NELLY. And I brought you a little laying pullet – boiled
and all she is – was crushed at the fall of night by the
curate's car. Feel the fat of that breast, Mister.

CHRISTY. It's bursting, surely. *(He feels it with the back*
5 *of his left hand, in which he holds the presents.)*

SARA. Will you pinch it? Is your right hand too sacred
for to use at all? *(She slips round behind him.)* It's a
glass he has. Well I never seen to this day, a man with
a looking-glass held to his back. Them that kills their
10 fathers is a vain lot surely.
    (Girls giggle.)

CHRISTY *(smiling innocently and piling presents on glass)*.
    I'm very thankful to you all to-day. . . .

WIDOW QUIN *(coming in quickly, at door)*. Sara Tansey,
15 Susan Brady, Honor Blake! What in glory has you
here at this hour of day?

GIRLS *(giggling)*. That's the man killed his father.

WIDOW QUIN *(coming to them)*. I know well it's the man;
and I'm after putting him down in the sports below
20 for racing, lepping, pitching, and the Lord knows
what.

SARA *(exuberantly)*. That's right, Widow Quin. I'll bet
my dowry that he'll lick the world.

WIDOW QUIN. If you will, you'd have a right to have him

---

1 **laying pullet:** junge Legehenne.
2 **to crush:** erdrücken.
3 **curate:** in Irland wie in England Hilfsgeistlicher, Vikar.
6 **Will you pinch it?:** Wollen Sie hineinkneifen?
10 **vain:** eitel, eingebildet.
11 **to giggle:** kichern.
20 **to pitch:** werfen.
22 **exuberantly** (adv.): überschwenglich.
22f. **I'll bet my dowry:** ich wette meine Aussteuer.
23 **to lick:** besiegen.

fresh and nourished in place of nursing a feast. *(Taking presents.)* Are you fasting or fed, young fellow?

CHRISTY. Fasting, if you please.

WIDOW QUIN *(loudly)*. Well, you're the lot. Stir up now
5 and give him his breakfast. *(To Christy.)* Come here
to me *(she puts him on bench beside her while the girls make tea and get his breakfast)* and let you tell us your story before Pegeen will come, in place of grinning your ears off like the moon of May.

10 CHRISTY *(beginning to be pleased)*. It's a long story you'd be destroyed listening.

WIDOW QUIN. Don't be letting on to be shy, a fine, gamey, treacherous lad the like of you. Was it in your house beyond you cracked his skull?

15 CHRISTY *(shy, but flattered)*. It was not. We were digging spuds in his cold, sloping, stony divil's patch of a field.

WIDOW QUIN. And you went asking money of him, or making talk of getting a wife would drive him from
20 his farm?

CHRISTY. I did not, then; but there I was, digging and digging, and "You squinting idiot," says he, "let you walk down now and tell the priest you'll wed the Widow Casey in a score of days."

---

1 **to nourish:** füttern, ernähren.
2 **Are you fasting or fed:** bist du noch nüchtern oder hast du schon was bekommen? *(to fast:* fasten.)
4 **you're the lot:** ihr seid mir welche.
8 f. **to grin one's ears off:** die Ohren vom Kopf grinsen.
13 **gamey:** mutig, tapfer.
   treacherous: verräterisch, treulos.
14 **to crack:** spalten.
16 **sloping:** schräg, abschüssig.
22 **squinting:** scheel, schielend.

WIDOW QUIN. And what kind was she?

CHRISTY *(with horror)*. A walking terror from beyond
the hills, and she two score and five years, and two
hundredweights and five pounds in the weighing
5 scales, with a limping leg on her, and a blinded eye,
and she a woman of noted misbehaviour with the old
and young. *(He begins gnawing a chicken leg.)*

GIRLS *(clustering round him, serving him)*. Glory be!

WIDOW QUIN. And what did he want driving you to wed
10 with her? *(She takes a bit of the chicken.)*

CHRISTY *(eating with growing satisfaction)*. He was letting on I was wanting a protector from the harshness
of the world, and he without a thought the whole
while but how he'd have her hut to live in and her
15 gold to drink.

WIDOW QUIN. There's maybe worse than a dry hearth and
a widow woman and your glass at night. So you hit
him then?

CHRISTY *(getting almost excited)*. I did not. "I won't wed
20 her," says I, "when all know she did suckle me for six
weeks when I came into the world, and she a hag this
day with a tongue on her has the crows and seabirds
scattered, the way they wouldn't cast a shadow on her
garden with the dread of her curse."

1 **what kind was she?:** was für eine war sie?
4f. **weighing scales:** Waagschalen.
5 **limping leg:** Hinkebein.
6 **of noted misbehaviour:** etwa: berüchtigt für ihren Lebenswandel.
8 **to cluster round:** (im Haufen) umdrängen.
12 **harshness:** Härte, Rauheit.
13f. **to be without a thought but:** keinen andern Gedanken haben als.
20 **to suckle:** säugen.
21 **hag:** Hexe.
24 **dread:** Furcht, Schrecken.

WIDOW QUIN *(teasingly)*. That one should be right company!

SARA *(eagerly)*. Don't mind her. Did you kill him then?

CHRISTY. "She's too good for the like of you," says he,
5   "and go on now or I'll flatten you out like a crawling
beast has passed under a dray." "You will not if I can
help it," says I. "Go on," says he, "or I'll have the
divil making garters of your limbs to-night." "You
will not if I can help it," says I. *(He sits bolt up,*
10   *brandishing his mug.)*

SARA. You were right surely.

CHRISTY *(impressively)*. With that the sun came out
between the cloud and the hill, and it shining green in
my face. "God have mercy on your soul," says he,
15   lifting a scythe; "or on your own," says I, raising the
loy.

SUSAN. That's a grand story.

HONOR. He tells it lovely.

CHRISTY *(flattered and confident, waving bone)*. He gave
20   a drive with the scythe, and I gave a lep to the east.
Then I turned around with my back to the north, and
I hit a blow on the ridge of his skull, laid him
stretched out, and he split to the knob of his gullet.
(He raises the chicken bone to his Adam's apple.)

3 **eagerly** (adv.): eifrig, begierig, ungeduldig.
5 **to flatten:** platt schlagen, glatt drücken.
5f. **crawling beast:** Kriechtier.
6 **dray:** Bierwagen.
8 **garter:** Strumpfband, Hosenband.
9 **bolt:** (kerzen)gerade.
10 **to brandish:** schwenken, schwingen.
15 **scythe:** Sense.
20 **drive:** Schlag, Stoß.
23 **knob of the gullet:** Kehlkopf, Adamsapfel (*gullet:* Speiseröhre).

GIRLS *(together)*. Well, you're a marvel! Oh, God bless
you! You're the lad surely!

SUSAN. I'm thinking the Lord God sent him this road to
make a second husband to the Widow Quin, and she
5 with a great yearning to be wedded though all dread
her here. Lift him on her knee, Sara Tansey.

WIDOW QUIN. Don't tease him.

SARA *(going over to dresser and counter very quickly,
and getting two glasses and porter)*. You're heroes
10 surely, and let you drink a supeen with your arms
linked like the outlandish lovers in the sailor's song.
(She links their arms and gives them the glasses.)
There now. Drink a health to the wonders of the
western world, the pirates, preachers, poteen-mak-
15 ers, with the jobbing jockies, parching peelers, and
the juries fill their stomachs selling judgments of the
English law. *(Brandishing the bottle.)*

WIDOW QUIN. That's a right toast, Sara Tansey. Now
Christy.

20 *(They drink with their arms linked, he drinking with
his left hand, she with her right. As they are drinking,
Pegeen Mike comes in with a milk can and stands
aghast. They all spring away from Christy. He goes
down left. Widow Quin remains seated.)*

25 PEGEEN *(angrily)*. What is it you're wanting *(to Sara)*?

---

1 **marvel:** Wunder.
5 **yearning:** Sehnsucht, Verlangen.
10 **supeen** (ir.): kleiner Schluck.
11 **to link:** verbinden, einhaken.
   outlandish: ausländisch.
15 **jobbing jockies:** Pferdehändler, die als Zwischenhändler agieren.
   parching: durstig, ausgedörrt, schmachtend.
23 **aghast:** entsetzt, starr.

SARA *(twisting her apron)*. An ounce of tobacco.

PEGEEN. Have you tuppence?

SARA. I've forgotten my purse.

PEGEEN. Then you'd best be getting it and not be fooling
5   us her. *(To the Widow Quin, with more elaborate
scorn.)* And what is it you're wanting, Widow Quin?

WIDOW QUIN *(insolently)*. A penn'orth of starch.

PEGEEN *(breaking out)*. And you without a white shift or
a shirt in your whole family since the drying of the
10   flood. I've no starch for the like of you, and let you
walk on now to Killamuck.

WIDOW QUIN *(turning to Christy, as she goes out with the
girls)*. Well, you're mighty huffy this day, Pegeen
Mike, and you young fellow, let you not forget the
15   sports and racing when the noon is by. *(They go out.)*

PEGEEN *(imperiously)*. Fling out that rubbish and put
them cups away. *(Christy tidies away in great haste.)*
Shove in the bench by the wall. *(He does so.)* And
hang that glass on the nail. What disturbed it at all?

---

1 **ounce:** Unze.
2 **tuppence** (= *two-pence*): 2 Pence.
3 **purse:** (Geld-)Börse.
5 **elaborate:** hier: betont.
7 **a penn'orth** (= *pennyworth*) **of starch:** für einen Penny Stärke.
8 **to break out:** ausbrechen, explodieren.
   shift: (Frauen-)Unterhemd.
9f. **the flood:** Sintflut.
13 **huffy:** verschnupft, übelnehmerisch.
16 **imperiously** (adv.): gebieterisch.
   rubbish: Müll; Plunder.
17 **to tidy away:** auf-, wegräumen.
18 **to shove:** schieben.
19 **What disturbed it at all?:** Wieso ist er überhaupt von seiner Stelle
   weg?

CHRISTY *(very meekly)*. I was making myself decent only, and this a fine country for young lovely girls.

PEGEEN *(sharply)*. Whisht your talking of girls. *(Goes to
counter right.)*

5 CHRISTY. Wouldn't any wish to be decent in a place. . . .

PEGEEN. Whisht, I'm saying.

CHRISTY *(looks at her face for a moment with great
misgivings, then as a last effort, takes up a loy, and
goes towards her, with feigned assurance)*. It was with

10 a loy the like of that I killed my father.

PEGEEN *(still sharply)*. You've told me that story six
times since the dawn of day.

CHRISTY *(reproachfully)*. It's a queer thing you wouldn't
care to be hearing it and them girls after walking four

15 miles to be listening to me now.

PEGEEN *(turning round astonished)*. Four miles!

CHRISTY *(apologetically)*. Didn't himself say there were
only bona fides living in the place?

PEGEEN. It's bona fides by the road they are, but that lot

20 come over the river lepping the stones. It's not three
perches when you go like that and I was down this
morning looking on the papers the post-boy does
have in his bag *(with meaning and emphasis)*, for
there was great news this day, Christopher Mahon.

25 *(She goes into room left.)*

CHRISTY *(suspiciously)*. Is it news of my murder?

PEGEEN *(inside)*. Murder indeed!

CHRISTY *(loudly)*. A murdered da?

---

8 **misgiving:** böse Ahnung, Befürchtung.
9 **with feigned assurance:** mit vorgetäuschter Zuversicht.
13 **reproachfully** (adv.): vorwurfsvoll.
17 **apologetically** (adv.): entschuldigend, rechtfertigend.
20 **to lep the stones:** (ein Gewässer) über Schrittsteine überqueren.

PEGEEN *(coming in again and crossing right)*. There was
not, but a story filled half a page of the hanging of a
man. Ah, that should be a fearful end, young fellow,
and it worst of all for a man destroyed his da, for the
5   like of him would get small mercies, and when it's
dead he is, they'd put him in a narrow grave, with
cheap sacking wrapping him round, and pour down
quicklime on his head, the way you'd see a woman
pouring any frish-frash from a cup.

10 CHRISTY *(very miserably)*. Oh, God help me. Are you
thinking I'm safe? You were saying at the fall of
night, I was shut of jeopardy and I here with yourselves.

PEGEEN *(severely)*. You'll be shut of jeopardy no place if
15   you go talking with a pack of wild girls the like of
them, do be walking abroad with the peelers, talking
whispers at the fall of night.

CHRISTY *(with terror)*. And you're thinking they'd tell?

PEGEEN *(with mock sympathy)*. Who knows, God help
20   you.

CHRISTY *(loudly)*. What joy would they have to bring
hanging to the likes of me?

PEGEEN. It's queer joys they have, and who knows the
thing they'd do, if it'd make the green stones cry itself
25   to think of you swaying and swiggling at the butt of a
rope, and you with a fine, stout neck, God bless you!

---

7 **to wrap round:** ein-, umwickeln.
8 **quicklime:** ungelöschter Kalk.
9 **frish-frash:** schaumartige Substanz.
12 **jeopardy:** Gefährdung.
14 **severely** (adv.): streng.
25 **to sway:** schwingen.
   to swiggle: sich winden.
26 **stout:** tapfer, mannhaft.

the way you'd be a half an hour, in great anguish,
getting your death.

CHRISTY *(getting his boots and putting them on)*. If
there's that terror of them, it'd be best, maybe, I
went on wandering like Esau or Cain and Abel on the
sides of Neifin or the Erris Plain.

PEGEEN *(beginning to play with him)*. It would, maybe,
for I've heard the Circuit Judges this place is a
heartless crew.

CHRISTY *(bitterly)*. It's more than judges this place is a
heartless crew. *(Looking up at her.)* And isn't it a
poor thing to be starting again and I a lonesome
fellow will be looking out on women and girls the way
the needy fallen spirits do be looking on the Lord?

PEGEEN. What call have you to be that lonesome when
there's poor girls walking Mayo in their thousands
now?

CHRISTY *(grimly)*. It's well you know what call I have.
It's well you know it's a lonesome thing to be passing
small towns with the lights shining sideways when the
night is down, or going in strange places with a dog
nosing before you and a dog nosing behind, or drawn

---

1 **anguish:** Pein, Qual, Schmerz.
5 **Esau:** vgl. 1. Mose 36,6–8.
  Cain and Abel: vgl. 1. Mose 4,11–16.
6 **Neifin:** Berg in Mayo.
  Erris Plain: Die Halbinsel Erris im äußersten Nordwesten Mayos
  galt als besonders einsam.
8 **circuit judge:** Richter oder Verteidiger, der die Gerichtsbarkeit nicht
  von einem festen Standort aus, sondern auf Rundreisen durch den
  Gerichtsbezirk ausübt.
14 **needy:** bedürftig.
  fallen spirit: gefallener Engel.
22 **to nose:** schnuppern, schnüffeln.

to the cities where you'd hear a voice kissing and
talking deep love in every shadow of the ditch, and
you passing on with an empty hungry stomach failing
from your heart.

5 PEGEEN. I'm thinking you're an odd man, Christy
Mahon. The oddest walking fellow I ever set my eyes
on to this hour to-day.

CHRISTY. What would any be but odd men and they
living lonesome in the world?

10 PEGEEN. I'm not odd, and I'm my whole life with my
father only.

CHRISTY (*with infinite admiration*). How would a lovely
handsome woman the like of you be lonesome when
all men should be thronging around to hear the

15 sweetness of your voice, and the little infant children
should be pestering your steps I'm thinking, and you
walking the roads.

PEGEEN. I'm hard set to know what way a coaxing fellow
the like of yourself should be lonesome either.

20 CHRISTY. Coaxing!

PEGEEN. Would you have me think a man never talked
with the girls would have the words you've spoken to-
day? It's only letting on you are to be lonesome, the
way you'd get around me now.

25 CHRISTY. I wish to God I was letting on; but I was
lonesome all times and born lonesome, I'm thinking,
as the moon of dawn. (*Going to door.*)

PEGEEN (*puzzled by his talk*). Well, it's a story I'm not

---

5 **odd:** merkwürdig, sonderbar.
14 **to throng:** sich drängen.
16 **to pester:** plagen, belästigen.
18 **to coax:** schmeicheln, beschwatzen.
24 **to get around:** herumkriegen.

understanding at all why you'd be worse than
another, Christy Mahon, and you a fine lad with the
great savagery to destroy your da.

CHRISTY. It's little I'm understanding myself, saving only
5   that my heart's scalded this day, and I going off
stretching out the earth between us, the way I'll not
be waking near you another dawn of the year till the
two of us do arise to hope or judgment with the saints
of God, and now I'd best be going with my wattle in
10   my hand, for hanging is a poor thing *(turning to go)*,
and it's little welcome only is left me in this house to-
day.

PEGEEN *(sharply)*. Christy! *(He turns round.)* Come here
to me. *(He goes towards her.)* Lay down that switch
15   and throw some sods on the fire. You're pot-boy in
this place, and I'll not have you mitch off from us
now.

CHRISTY. You were saying I'd be hanged if I stay.

PEGEEN *(quite kindly at last)*. I'm after going down and
20   reading the fearful crimes of Ireland for two weeks or
three, and there wasn't a word of your murder.
(Getting up and going over to the counter.) They've
likely not found the body. You're safe so with ourselves.

25 CHRISTY *(astonished, slowly)*. It's making game of me
you were *(following her with fearful joy)*, and I can
stay so, working at your side, and I not lonesome
from this mortal day.

---

3 **savagery:** Wildheit.
5 **to scald:** verbrühen, verbrennen.
9 **wattle:** kleine Rute.
14 **switch:** Rute.
15 **sod:** Stück Torf.
16 **to mitch off** (dial.): davonschleichen, sich drücken.

PEGEEN. What's to hinder you staying, except the widow
woman or the young girls would inveigle you off?

CHRISTY *(with rapture)*. And I'll have your words from
this day filling my ears, and that look is come upon
5 you meeting my two eyes, and I watching you loafing
around in the warm sun, or rinsing your ankles when
the night is come.

PEGEEN *(kindly, but a little embarrassed)*. I'm thinking
you'll be a loyal young lad to have working around,
10 and if you vexed me a while since with your leaguing
with the girls, I wouldn't give a thraneen for a lad
hadn't a mighty spirit in him and a gamey heart.
*(Shawn Keogh runs in carrying a cleeve on his back,
followed by the Widow Quin.)*

15 SHAWN *(to Pegeen)*. I was passing below and I seen your
mountainy sheep eating cabbages in Jimmy's field.
Run up or they'll be bursting surely.

PEGEEN. Oh, God mend them! *(She puts a shawl over her
head and runs out.)*

20 CHRISTY *(looking from one to the other, still in high
spirits)*. I'd best go to her aid maybe. I'm handy with
ewes.

WIDOW QUIN *(closing the door)*. She can do that much,
and there is Shaneen has long speeches for to tell you
25 now. *(She sits down with an amused smile.)*

---

2 **to inveigle:** locken, verleiten, verführen.
3 **rapture:** Entzückung.
5 f. **to loaf around:** herumlungern, bummeln.
10 **to vex:** quälen.
   to league: sich verbünden.
11 **thraneen** (ir.): Strohhalm.
13 **cleeve** (ir.): Korb.
21 **handy:** geschickt.

SHAWN *(taking something from his pocket and offering it to Christy)*. Do you see that, Mister?

CHRISTY *(looking at it)*. The half of a ticket to the Western States!

5 SHAWN *(trembling with anxiety)*. I'll give it to you and my new hat *(pulling it out of hamper)*; and my breeches with the double seat *(pulling it out)*; and my new coat is woven from the blackest shearings for three miles around *(giving him the coat)*; I'll give you the whole

10 of them and my blessing and the blessing of Father Reilly itself, maybe, if you'll quit from this and leave us in the peace we had till last night at the fall of dark.

CHRISTY *(with a new arrogance)*. And for what is it you're wanting to get shut of me?

15 SHAWN *(looking to the Widow for help)*. I'm a poor scholar with middling faculties to coin a lie, so I'll tell you the truth, Christy Mahon. I'm wedding with Pegeen beyond, and I don't think well of having a clever fearless man the like of you dwelling in her

20 house.

CHRISTY *(almost pugnaciously)*. And you'd be using bribery for to banish me?

SHAWN *(in a imploring voice)*. Let you not take it badly, mister honey, isn't beyond the best place for you

25 where you'll have golden chains and shiny coats and

---

6 **hamper:** Packkorb, Eßkorb.
  breeches (pl.): Reithose.
8 **shearings** (pl.): Scherwolle.
14 **to get shut of s.o.:** jdn. loswerden.
16 **to coin:** erfinden.
21 **pugnaciously** (adv.): kampflustig, streitsüchtig.
22 **bribery:** Bestechung.
23 **to implore:** (an)flehen.

you riding upon hunters with the ladies of the land.
*(He makes an eager sign to the Widow Quin to come
to help him.)*

WIDOW QUIN *(coming over)*. It's true for him, and you'd
5   best quit off and not have that poor girl setting her
mind on you, for there's Shaneen thinks she wouldn't
suit you though all is saying that she'll wed you now.
(Christy beams with delight.)

SHAWN *(in terrified earnest)*. She wouldn't suit you, and
10   she with the divil's own temper the way you'd be
strangling one another in a score of days. *(He makes
the movement of strangling with his hands.)* It's the
like of me only that she's fit for, a quiet simple fellow
wouldn't raise a hand upon her if she scratched itself.

15   WIDOW QUIN *(putting Shawn's hat on Christy)*. Fit them
clothes on you anyhow, young fellow, and he'd
maybe loan them to you for the sports. *(Pushing him
towards inner door.)* Fit them on and you can give
your answer when you have them tried.

20   CHRISTY *(beaming, delighted with the clothes)*. I will
then, I'd like herself to see me in them tweeds and
hat. *(He goes into room and shuts the door.)*

SHAWN *(in great anxiety)*. He'd like herself to see them!
He'll not leave us, Widow Quin. He's a score of divils
25   in him, the way it's well nigh certain he will wed
Pegeen.

---

1 **hunter:** Jagdpferd.
8 **to beam:** strahlen, glänzen.
11 **to strangle:** erwürgen.
14 **to scratch:** kratzen.
21 **tweeds:** Tweedsachen (Kleidung aus Tweed, einem englischen Woll-
stoff).
23 **anxiety:** Besorgnis, Angst.

WIDOW QUIN *(jeeringly)*. It's true all girls are fond of
courage and do hate the like of you.

SHAWN *(walking about in desperation)*. Oh, Widow
Quin, what'll I be doing now? I'd inform again him,
but he'd burst from Kilmainham and he'd be sure and
certain to destroy me. If I wasn't so God-fearing, I'd
near have courage to come behind him and run a pike
into his side. Oh, it's a hard case to be an orphan and
not to have your father that you're used to, and you'd
easy kill and make yourself a hero in the sight of all.
(Coming up to her.) Oh, Widow Quin, will you find
me some contrivance when I've promised you a ewe?

WIDOW QUIN. A ewe's a small thing, but what would you
give me if I did wed him and did save you so?

SHAWN *(with astonishment)*. You!

WIDOW QUIN. Aye. Would you give me the red cow you
have and the mountainy ram, and the right of way
across your rye path, and a load of dung at Michaelmas, and turbary upon the western hill?

SHAWN *(radiant with hope)*. I would surely, and I'd give
you the wedding-ring I have, and the loan of the new
suit, the way you'd have him decent on the wedding-
day. I'd give you two kids for your dinner and a

5

0

5

0

---

  4 **to inform:** anzeigen.
  5 **Kilmainham:** bekanntes Gefängnis in Dublin.
  7 **pike** (dial.): Heugabel.
  8 **orphan:** Waisenkind.
 12 **contrivance:** Kunstgriff, Kniff, List.
 17 **right of way:** Wegerecht.
 18 **rye path:** Weg entlang des Roggenfeldes.
 18 f. **Michaelmas:** Michaelstag (29. September).
 19 **turbary:** Recht, auf fremdem Land Torf zu stechen.
 20 **radiant:** strahlend.
 23 **kid:** Zicklein.

gallon of poteen, and I'd call the piper on the long car
to your wedding from Crossmolina or from Ballina.
I'd give you. . .

WIDOW QUIN. That'll do, so, and let you whisht, for he's
5   coming now again.

   (*Christy comes in very natty in the new clothes. Widow
   Quin goes to him admiringly.*)

WIDOW QUIN. If you seen yourself now, I'm thinking
   you'd be too proud to speak to us at all, and it'd be a
10   pity surely to have your like sailing from Mayo to the
   Western World.

CHRISTY (*as proud as a peacock*). I'm not going. If this is
   a poor place itself, I'll make myself contented to be
   lodging here.

15   (*Widow Quin makes a sign to Shawn to leave them.*)

SHAWN. Well, I'm going measuring the race-course while
   the tide is low, so I'll leave you the garments and my
   blessing for the sports to-day. God bless you! (*He
   wriggles out.*)

20 WIDOW QUIN (*admiring Christy*). Well you're mighty
   spruce, young fellow. Sit down now while you're
   quiet till you talk with me.

CHRISTY (*swaggering*). I'm going abroad on the hillside
   for to seek Pegeen.

25 WIDOW QUIN. You'll have time and plenty for to seek
   Pegeen, and you heard me saying at the fall of night
   the two of us should be great company.

CHRISTY. From this out I'll have no want of company

---

 1 **gallon:** Gallone (Hohlmaß, 4,55 l).
 6 **natty:** schmuck, geputzt.
12 **peacock:** Pfau.
21 **spruce:** schmuck, geschniegelt.
23 **to swagger:** einherstolzieren, großtun, prahlen.

when all sorts is bringing me their food and clothing
(he swaggers to the door, tightening his belt), the way
they'd set their eyes upon a gallant orphan cleft his
father with one blow to the breeches belt. *(He opens
door, then staggers back.)* Saints of glory! Holy angels
from the throne of light!

WIDOW QUIN *(going over)*. What ails you?

CHRISTY. It's the walking spirit of my murdered da!

WIDOW QUIN *(looking out)*. Is it that tramper?

CHRISTY *(wildly)*. Where'll I hide my poor body from
that ghost of hell?
*(The door is pushed open, and Old Mahon appears on
threshold. Christy darts in behind door.)*

WIDOW QUIN *(in great amusement)*. God save you, my
poor man.

MAHON *(gruffly)*. Did you see a young lad passing this
way in the early morning or the fall of night?

WIDOW QUIN. You're a queer kind to walk in not saluting
at all.

MAHON. Did you see the young lad?

WIDOW QUIN *(stiffly)*. What kind was he?

MAHON. An ugly young streeler with a murderous gob
on him and a little switch in his hand. I met a tramper
seen him coming this way at the fall of night.

WIDOW QUIN. There's harvest hundreds do be passing

---

2 **to tighten:** enger schnallen, festziehen.
3 **gallant:** stattlich; tapfer.
   to cleave: spalten.
5 **to stagger:** wanken, schwanken, taumeln.
9 **tramper:** *tramp*.
13 **threshold:** (Tür-)Schwelle.
   to dart in: (in Deckung) springen, stürzen.
22 **streeler** (ir.): Bummler, Faulenzer.
   gob (slang): Fresse, Maul.

these days for the Sligo boat. For what is it you're
wanting him, my poor man?

MAHON. I want to destroy him for breaking the head on
me with the clout of a loy. *(He takes off a big hat, and*
shows his head in a mass of bandages and plaster, with
some pride.) It was he did that, and amn't I a great
wonder to think I've traced him ten days with that
rent in my crown?

WIDOW QUIN *(taking his head in both hands and examin-*
ing it with extreme delight). That was a great blow.
And who hit you? A robber maybe?

MAHON. It was my own son hit me, and he the divil a
robber or anything else but a dirty, stuttering lout.

WIDOW QUIN *(letting go his skull and wiping her hands in*
her apron). You'd best be wary of a mortified scalp, I
think they call it, lepping around with that wound in
the splendour of the sun. It was a bad blow surely,
and you should have vexed him fearful to make him
strike that gash in his da.

MAHON. Is it me?

WIDOW QUIN *(amusing herself).* Aye. And isn't it a great
shame when the old and hardened do torment the
young?

MAHON *(raging).* Torment him is it? And I after holding
out with the patience of a martyred saint, till there's

---

4 **clout:** Schlag.
8 **rent:** Riß.
 crown: Scheitel.
13 **stuttering lout:** stotternder Lümmel, Tölpel.
15 **mortified:** brandig, abgestorben.
17 **splendour:** Glanz.
19 **gash:** klaffende Wunde.
22 **hardened:** abgehärtet, hartgesotten.

nothing but destruction on me and I'm driven out in
my old age with none to aid me?

WIDOW QUIN (*greatly amused*). It's a sacred wonder the
way that wickedness will spoil a man.

MAHON. My wickedness, is it? Amn't I after saying it is
himself has me destroyed, and he a lier on walls, a
talker of folly, a man you'd see stretched the half of
the day in the brown ferns with his belly to the sun.

WIDOW QUIN. Not working at all?

MAHON. The divil a work, or if he did itself, you'd see
him raising up a haystack like the stalk of a rush or
driving our last cow till he broke her leg at the hip,
and when he wasn't at that he'd be fooling over little
birds he had – finches and felts – or making mugs at
his own self in the bit of a glass we had hung on the
wall.

WIDOW QUIN (*looking at Christy*). What way was he so
foolish? It was running wild after the girls maybe?

MAHON (*with a shout of derision*). Running wild, is it? If
he seen a red petticoat coming swinging over the hill,
he'd be off to hide in the sticks, and you'd see him
shooting out his sheep's eyes between the little twigs

---

 4 **to spoil:** verziehen, verderben.
 6 **a lier on walls:** Gemeint ist ein Nichtstuer und Prahlhans.
 8 **fern:** Farn.
11 **a haystack like the stalk of a rush:** ein Heuhaufen wie ein Binsen-
halm.
14 **finch:** Fink.
 felt: Krammetsvogel.
 to make mugs: Gesichter schneiden.
19 **derision:** Spott, Hohn.
20 **petticoat:** Unterrock.
21 **sticks** (pl.): Gebüsch.

and leaves, and his two ears rising like a hare looking
out through a gap. Girls indeed!

WIDOW QUIN. It was drink maybe?

MAHON. And he a poor fellow would get drunk on the
5   smell of a pint! He'd a queer rotten stomach, I'm
telling you, and when I gave him three pulls from my
pipe a while since, he was taken with contortions till I
had to send him in the ass cart to the females' nurse.

WIDOW QUIN (*clasping her hands*). Well, I never till this
10 day heard tell of a man the like of that.

MAHON. I'd take a mighty oath you didn't surely, and
wasn't he the laughing joke of every female woman
where four baronies meet, the way the girls would
stop their weeding if they seen him coming the road
15 to let a roar at him, and call him the looney of Mahon's.

WIDOW QUIN. I'd give the world and all to see the like of
him. What kind was he?

MAHON. A small low fellow.

20 WIDOW QUIN. And dark?

MAHON. Dark and dirty.

WIDOW QUIN (*considering*). I'm thinking I seen him.

MAHON (*eagerly*). An ugly young blackguard?

WIDOW QUIN. A hideous, fearful villain, and the spit of
25 you.

---

5 **to rot:** verfaulen, verderben, verkommen.
7 **contortions:** Verdrehungen, Krämpfe.
9 **to clasp:** ergreifen, umklammern.
13 **barony** (ir.): Grafschaftsdistrikt.
15 **looney:** *lunatic:* Depp, Idiot.
23 **blackguard:** Lump, Schuft.
24 **hideous:** gräßlich, entsetzlich.
24 f. **the spit of you:** etwa: ganz euer Ebenbild.

MAHON. What way is he fled?

WIDOW QUIN. Gone over the hills to catch a coasting
steamer to the north or south.

MAHON. Could I pull up on him now?

5 WIDOW QUIN. If you'll cross the sands below where the
tide is out, you'll be in it as soon as himself, for he
had to go round ten miles by the top of the bay. *(She
points from the door.)* Strike down by the head
beyond and then follow on the roadway to the north
10 and east.

(Mahon goes abruptly.)

WIDOW QUIN *(shouting after him)*. Let you give him a
good vengeance when you come up with him, but
don't put yourself in the power of the law, for it'd be
15 a poor thing to see a judge in his black cap reading
out his sentence on a civil warrior the like of you.
*(She swings the door to and looks at Christy, who is
cowering in terror, for a moment, then she bursts into
a laugh.)* Well, you're the walking playboy of the
20 western world, and that's the poor man you had
divided to his breeches belt.

CHRISTY *(looking out; then, to her)*. What'll Pegeen say
when she hears that story? What'll she be saying to
me now?

25 WIDOW QUIN. She'll knock the head of you, I'm thinking,
and drive you from the door. God help her to be

2f. **coasting steamer:** Küstendampfer.
4 **to pull up on s.o.:** jdn. einholen.
6 **tide:** Flut.
13 **vengeance:** Strafe, Bestrafung.
16 **warrior:** Krieger, Kämpfer.
17 **to swing to:** zuschlagen.
18 **to cower:** kauern.

taking you for a wonder, and you a little schemer
making up a story you destroyed your da.

CHRISTY *(turning to the door, nearly speechless with rage,
half to himself).* To be letting on he was dead, and
5   coming back to his life, and following me like an old
weazel tracing a rat, and coming in here laying
desolation between my own self and the fine women
of Ireland, and he a kind of carcase that you'd fling
upon the sea. . . .

10   WIDOW QUIN *(more soberly).* There's talking for a man's
one only son.

CHRISTY *(breaking out).* His one son, is it? May I meet
him with one tooth and it aching, and one eye to be
seeing seven and seventy divils in the twists of the
15   road, and one old timber leg on him to limp into the
scalding grave. *(Looking out.)* There he is now crossing the strands, and that the Lord God would send a
high wave to wash him from the world.

WIDOW QUIN *(scandalized).* Have you no shame? *(Putt-
20   ing her hand on his shoulder and turning him round.)*
What ails you? Near crying, is it?

CHRISTY *(in despair and grief).* Amn't I after seeing the
love-light of the star of knowledge shining from her
brow, and hearing words would put you thinking on
25   the holy Brigid speaking to the infant saints, and now
she'll be turning again, and speaking hard words to
me, like an old woman with a spavindy ass she'd
have, urging on a hill.

---

1 **schemer:** Ränkeschmied.
6 **weazel:** Wiesel.
10 **soberly** (adv.): nüchtern.
27 **spavindy:** spatig, lahm.
28 **to urge:** antreiben.

WIDOW QUIN. There's poetry talk for a girl you'd see
itching and scratching, and she with a stale stink of
poteen on her from selling in the shop.

CHRISTY *(impatiently)*. It's her like is fitted to be handl-
ing merchandise in the heavens above, and what'll I
be doing now, I ask you, and I a kind of wonder was
jilted by the heavens when a day was by.

*(There is a distant noise of girls' voices. Widow Quin
looks from window and comes to him, hurriedly.)*

WIDOW QUIN. You'll be doing like myself, I'm thinking,
when I did destroy my man, for I'm above many's the
day, odd times in great spirits, abroad in the sunshine, darning a stocking or stitching a shift, and odd
times again looking out on the schooners, hookers,
trawlers is sailing the sea, and I thinking on the
gallant hairy fellows are drifting beyond, and myself
long years living alone.

CHRISTY *(interested)*. You're like me, so.

WIDOW QUIN. I am your like, and it's for that I'm taking a
fancy to you, and I with my little houseen above
where there'd be myself to tend you, and none to ask
were you a murderer or what at all.

CHRISTY. And what would I be doing if I left Pegeen?

WIDOW QUIN. I've nice jobs you could be doing, gather-

2 **to itch:** (sich) jucken.
  stale: schal, abgestanden.
7 **to jilt:** narren, betrügen.
13 **to darn:** stopfen, flicken.
14 **schooner:** Schoner (mehrmastiges Segelschiff).
  hooker: Huker (größeres Fischerboot).
15 **trawler:** Schlepper, Schleppkahn.
19 f. **to take a fancy to s.o.:** jdn. mögen, für jdn. etwas übrig haben.
21 **to tend:** sorgen, versorgen.

ing shells to make a whitewash for our hut within,
building up a little goose-house, or stretching a new
skin on an old curagh I have, and if my hut is far from
all sides, it's there you'll meet the wisest old men, I
tell you, at the corner of my wheel, and it's there
yourself and me will have great times whispering and
hugging . . .

VOICES *(outside, calling far away).* Christy! Christy Mahon! Christy!

CHRISTY. Is it Pegeen Mike?

WIDOW QUIN. It's the young girls, I'm thinking, coming
to bring you to the sports below, and what is it you'll
have me to tell them now?

CHRISTY. Aid me for to win Pegeen. It's herself only that
I'm seeking now. *(Widow Quin gets up and goes to
window.)* Aid me for to win her, and I'll be asking
God to stretch a hand to you in the hour of death, and
lead you short cuts through the Meadows of Ease, and
up the floor of Heaven to the Footstool of the
Virgin's Son.

WIDOW QUIN. There's praying!

VOICES *(nearer).* Christy! Christy Mahon!

CHRISTY *(with agitation).* They're coming. Will you
swear to aid and save me for the love of Christ?

WIDOW QUIN *(looks at him for a moment).* If I aid you,
will you swear to give me a right of way I want, and a

---

 1 **whitewash:** Tünche.
 3 **curagh:** Ruderboot, dessen leichter Holzrahmen mit Tierhäuten
    oder geteerter Leinwand überspannt ist.
 5 **wheel:** *spinning-wheel:* Spinnrad.
 7 **to hug:** umarmen, lieben.
18 **ease:** Behaglichkeit.
19 **footstool:** Fußschemel.
23 **agitation:** Erregtheit.

mountainy ram, and a load of dung at Michaelmas,
the time that you'll be master here?

CHRISTY. I will, by the elements and stars of night.

WIDOW QUIN. Then we'll not say a word of the old fellow,
the way Pegeen won't know your story till the end of
time.

CHRISTY. And if he chances to return again?

WIDOW QUIN. We'll swear he's a maniac and not your da.
I could take an oath I seen him raving on the sands to-
day.

(Girls run in.)

SUSAN. Come on to the sports below. Pegeen says you're
to come.

SARA TANSEY. The lepping's beginning, and we've a
jockey's suit to fit upon you for the mule race on the
sands below.

HONOR. Come on, will you.

CHRISTY. I will then if Pegeen's beyond.

SARA. She's in the boreen making game of Shaneen
Keogh.

CHRISTY. Then I'll be going to her now. *(He runs out,
followed by the Girls.)*

WIDOW QUIN. Well, if the worst comes in the end of all,
it'll be great game to see there's none to pity him but
a widow woman, the like of me, has buried her
children and destroyed her man. *(She goes out.)*

CURTAIN

---

8 **maniac:** Irrer, Wahnsinniger.
9 **to rave:** rasen, toben.
15 **mule:** Maulesel.
19 **boreen** (ir.): schmale Gasse, unbefestigter Weg.

Act III

Scene, as before. Later in the day. Jimmy comes in, slightly drunk.

JIMMY *(calls)*. Pegeen! *(Crosses to inner door.)* Pegeen
5   Mike! *(Comes back again into the room.)* Pegeen!
    (Philly comes in in the same state.) (To Philly.) Did
    you see herself?
PHILLY. I did not; but I sent Shawn Keogh with the ass
    cart for to bear him home. *(Trying cupboards which
10   are locked.)* Well, isn't he a nasty man to get into such
    staggers at a morning wake, and isn't herself the
    divil's daughter for locking, and she so fussy after that
    young gaffer, you might take your death with drought
    and none to heed you.
15 JIMMY. It's little wonder she'd be fussy, and he after
    bringing bankrupt ruin on the roulette man, and the
    trick-o'-the-loop man, and breaking the nose of the
    cockshot-man, and winning all in the sports below,
    racing, lepping, dancing, and the Lord knows what!
20   He's right luck, I'm telling you.

3 **slightly** (adv.): leicht.
11 **stagger:** Schwanken, Taumeln.
12 **to be fussy after s.o.:** um jdn. viel Aufhebens machen; auf jdn.
    scharf sein.
13 **gaffer:** Flegel, Schwätzer.
    drought: Trockenheit, Dürre, gemeint ist hier: Durst.
17 **trick-o'-the-loop:** Ringwerfen.
18 **cockshot:** Hahnenschlagen.

PHILLY. If he has he'll be rightly hobbled yet, and he not
able to say ten words without making a brag of the
way he killed his father and the great blow he hit with
the loy.

5 JIMMY. A man can't hang by his own informing, and his
father should be rotten by now.
(Old Mahon passes window slowly.)

PHILLY. Supposing a man's digging spuds in that field
with a long spade, and supposing he flings up the two

10 halves of that skull, what'll be said then in the papers
and the courts of law?

JIMMY. They'd say it was an old Dane, maybe, was
drowned in the flood. *(Old Mahon comes in and sits
down near door listening.)* Did you never hear tell of

15 the skulls they have in the city of Dublin, ranged out
like blue jugs in a cabin of Connaught?

PHILLY. And you believe that?

JIMMY *(pugnaciously)*. Didn't a lad see them and he after
coming from harvesting in the Liverpool boat? "They

20 have them there," says he, "making a show of the
great people there was one time walking the world.
White skulls and black skulls and yellow skulls, and
some with full teeth and some haven't only but one."

PHILLY. It was no lie, maybe, for when I was a young

25 lad, there was a graveyard beyond the house with the
remnants of a man who had thighs as long as your
arm. He was a horrid man, I'm telling you, and there
was many a fine Sunday I'd put him together for fun,

---

1 **to be hobbled:** eine Niederlage erleiden, in Verlegenheit kommen.
2 **brag:** Prahlen.
15 **to range out:** aufreihen, in einer Reihe aufstellen.
26 **remnants:** Überreste.
   thigh: Oberschenkel.

and he with shiny bones you wouldn't meet the like of
these days in the cities of the world.

MAHON *(getting up).* You wouldn't is it? Lay your eyes
on that skull, and tell me where and when there was
5   another the like of it, is splintered only from the blow
of a loy.

PHILLY. Glory be to God! And who hit you at all?

MAHON *(triumphantly).* It was my own son hit me.
Would you believe that?

10 JIMMY. Well there's wonders hidden in the heart of man!

PHILLY *(suspiciously).* And what way was it done?

MAHON *(wandering about the room).* I'm after walking
hundreds and long scores of miles, winning clean
beds and the fill of my belly four times in the day, and
15   I doing nothing but telling stories of that naked truth.
(He comes to them a little aggressively.) Give me a
supeen and I'll tell you now.
*(Widow Quin comes in and stands aghast behind him.
He is facing Jimmy and Philly, who are on the left.)*

20 JIMMY. Ask herself beyond. She's the stuff hidden in her
shawl.

WIDOW QUIN *(coming to Mahon quickly).* You here, is it?
You didn't go far at all?

MAHON. I seen the coasting steamer passing, and I got a
25   drought upon me and a cramping leg, so I said, "The
divil go along with him," and turned again. *(Looking
under her shawl.)* And let you give me a supeen, for
I'm destroyed travelling since Tuesday was a week.

WIDOW QUIN *(getting a glass, in a cajoling tone).* Sit down

---

5 **to splinter:** splittern.
25 **cramping leg:** krampfendes Bein, Krampf im Bein.
29 **to cajole:** schmeicheln, um den Bart gehen.

then by the fire and take your ease for a space.
You've a right to be destroyed indeed, with your
walking, and fighting, and facing the sun *(giving him
poteen from a stone jar she has brought in)*. There
now is a drink for you, and may it be to your
happiness and length of life.

MAHON *(taking glass greedily, and sitting down by fire)*.
God increase you!

WIDOW QUIN *(taking men to the right stealthily)*. Do you
know what? That man's raving from his wound to-
day, for I met him a while since telling a rambling tale
of a tinker had him destroyed. Then he heard of
Christy's deed, and he up and says it was his son had
cracked his skull. Oh, isn't madness a fright, for he'll
go killing someone yet and he thinking it's the man
has struck him so!

JIMMY *(entirely convinced)*. It's a fright surely. I knew a
party was kicked in the head by a red mare, and he
went killing horses a great while, till he eat the insides
of a clock and died after.

PHILLY *(with suspicion)*. Did he see Christy?

WIDOW QUIN. He didn't. *(With a warning gesture.)* Let
you not be putting him in mind of him, or you'll be
likely summoned if there's murder done. *(Looking
round at Mahon.)* Whisht! He's listening. Wait now
till you hear me taking him easy and unravelling all.

---

4 **jar:** Krug, irdenes Gefäß.
11 **rambling tale:** zusammenhanglose Geschichte.
14 **fright:** Schreckbild, Graus.
17f. **a party:** jemand.
18 **mare:** Stute.
24 **to summon:** vor Gericht laden, vorladen.
26 **to unravel:** entwirren, auflösen.

(She goes to Mahon.) And what way are you feeling,
Mister? Are you in contentment now?

MAHON *(slightly emotional from his drink).* I'm poorly
only, for it's a hard story the way I'm left to-day,
5   when it was I did tend him from his hour of birth, and
he a dunce never reached his second book, the way
he'd come from school, many's the day, with his legs
lamed under him, and he blackened with his beatings
like a tinker's ass. It's a hard story, I'm saying, the
10   way some do have their next and nighest raising up a
hand of murder on them, and some is lonesome
getting their death with lamentation in the dead of
night.

WIDOW QUIN *(not knowing what to say).* To hear you
15   talking so quiet, who'd know you were the same
fellow we seen pass to-day?

MAHON. I'm the same surely. The wrack and ruin of
three score years; and it's a terror to live that length, I
tell you, and to have your sons going to the dogs
20   against you, and you wore out scolding them, and
skelping them, and God knows what.

PHILLY *(to Jimmy).* He's not raving. *(To Widow Quin.)*
Will you ask him what kind was his son?

WIDOW QUIN *(to Mahon, with a peculiar look).* Was your
25   son that hit you a lad of one year and a score maybe,
a great hand at racing and lepping and licking the
world?

MAHON *(turning on her with a roar of rage).* Didn't you
hear me say he was the fool of men, the way from this

---

17 **wrack:** Untergang, Ruin.
21 **to skelp:** prügeln, schlagen.
26 **to be a great hand at s.th.:** sehr geübt in etwas sein.

out he'll know the orphan's lot with old and young
making game of him and they swearing, raging, kicking at him like a mangy cur.
(A great burst of cheering outside, some way off.)

5 MAHON *(putting his hands to his ears)*. What in the name
of God do they want roaring below?

WIDOW QUIN *(with the shade of a smile)*. They're cheering
a young lad, the champion playboy of the western
world.

10 *(More cheering.)*

MAHON *(going to window)*. It'd split my heart to hear
them, and I with pulses in my brain-pan for a week
gone by. Is it racing they are?

JIMMY *(looking from door)*. It is then. They are mount-
15 ing him for the mule race will be run upon the sands.
That's the playboy on the winkered mule.

MAHON *(puzzled)*. That lad, is it? If you said it was a fool
he was, I'd have laid a mighty oath he was the
likeness of my wandering son. *(Philly nods at Jimmy.*
20 *Mahon, uneasily, putting his hand to his head.)* Faith,
I'm thinking I'll go walking for to view the race.

WIDOW QUIN *(stopping him, sharply)*. You will not.
You'd best take the road to Belmullet, and not be
dilly-dallying in this place where there isn't a spot you
25 could sleep.

---

1 **lot:** Los, Schicksal.
3 **mangy:** räudig, schmutzig.
  cur: *cur dog.*
4 **to cheer:** jubeln, Hurra rufen.
12 **pulse:** Pulsschlag, Pulshämmern.
  brain-pan: Hirnschale.
14 f. **to mount:** auf (ein Reittier) setzen.
16 **winkered:** *blinkered:* mit Scheuklappen versehen.
24 **to dilly-dally:** trödeln, zaudern.

PHILLY *(coming forward).* Don't mind her. Mount there
　　on the bench and you'll have a view of the whole.
　　They're hurrying before the tide will rise, and it'd be
　　near over if you went down the pathway through the
5　　crags below.

MAHON *(mounts on bench, Widow Quin beside him).*
　　That's a right view again the edge of the sea. They're
　　coming now from the point. He's leading. Who is he
　　at all?

10　WIDOW QUIN. He's the champion of the world I tell you,
　　and there isn't a hap'orth isn't falling lucky to his
　　hands to-day.

PHILLY *(looking out, interested in the race).* Look at that.
　　They're pressing him now.

15　JIMMY. He'll win it yet.

PHILLY. Take your time, Jimmy Farrell. It's too soon to
　　say.

WIDOW QUIN *(shouting).* Watch him taking the gate.
　　There's riding.

20　JIMMY *(cheering).* More power to the young lad!

MAHON. He's passing the third.

JIMMY. He'll lick them yet.

WIDOW QUIN. He'd lick them if he was running races with
　　a score itself.

25　MAHON. Look at the mule he has kicking the stars.

WIDOW QUIN. There was a lep! *(Catching hold of Mahon*

---

5 **crag:** Klippe.
8f. **Who is he at all?:** Wer ist das überhaupt?
11 **hap'orth:** *halfpennyworth:* für einen halben Penny; (fig.) kaum
　　etwas.
14 **to press:** bedrängen, antreiben, zusetzen.
20 **More power to the young lad!:** Weiter so!

in her excitement.) He's fallen! He's mounted again!
Faith, he's passing them all!

JIMMY. Look at him skelping her!

PHILLY. And the mountain girls hooshing him on!

5 JIMMY. It's the last turn! The post's cleared for them
now!

MAHON. Look at the narrow place. He'll be into the
bogs! (*With a yell.*) Good rider! He's through it again!

JIMMY. He's neck and neck!

10 MAHON. Good boy to him! Flames, but he's in!
(*Great cheering, in which all join.*)

MAHON (*with hesitation*). What's that? They're raising
him up. They're coming this way. (*With a roar of rage
and astonishment.*) It's Christy! by the stars of God!
15 I'd know his way of spitting and he astride the moon.
(*He jumps down and makes a run for the door, but
Widow Quin catches him and pulls him back.*)

WIDOW QUIN. Stay quiet, will you. That's not your son.
(*To Jimmy.*) Stop him, or you'll get a month for the
20 abetting of manslaughter and be fined as well.

JIMMY. I'll hold him.

MAHON (*struggling*). Let me out! Let me out the lot of
you! till I have my vengeance on his head to-day.

WIDOW QUIN (*shaking him, vehemently*). That's not your

---

1 **excitement:** Erregung, Aufregung.
4 **to hoosh s.o. on** (ir.): jdn. aufmuntern, anfeuern.
9 **He's neck and neck:** Er ist Kopf an Kopf.
10 **Good boy to him!:** Großartiger Kerl!
   Flames, but he's in!: Donnerwetter! Er ist ja schon drin.
12 **hesitation:** Zögern.
20 **abetting:** Anstiftung.
   manslaughter: Totschlag.
   to fine: zu einer Geldstrafe verurteilen.
24 **vehemently** (adv.): heftig, ungestüm.

son. That's a man is going to make a marriage with
the daughter of this house, a place with fine trade,
with a licence, and with poteen too.

MAHON (*amazed*). That man marrying a decent and a
5   moneyed girl! Is it mad yous are? Is it in a crazy-
house for females that I'm landed now?

WIDOW QUIN. It's mad yourself is with the blow upon
your head. That lad is the wonder of the western
world.

10   MAHON. I seen it's my son.

WIDOW QUIN. You seen that you're mad. (*Cheering outside.*) Do you hear them cheering him in the zig-zags
of the road? Aren't you after saying that your son's a
fool, and how would they be cheering a true idiot
15   born?

MAHON (*getting distressed*). It's maybe out of reason that
man's himself. (*Cheering again.*) There's none surely
will go cheering him. Oh, I'm raving with a madness
that would fright the world. (*He sits down with his
20   hand to his head.*) There was one time I seen ten
scarlet divils letting on they'd cork my spirit in a
gallon can; and one time I seen rats as big as badgers
sucking the life blood from the butt of my lug; but I
never till this day confused that dribbling idiot with a
25   likely man. I'm destroyed surely.

WIDOW QUIN. And who'd wonder when it's your brain-
pan that is gaping now?

---

16 **distressed:** bekümmert.
21 **to cork:** einkorken.
22 **badger:** Dachs.
23 **the butt of my lug:** mein Ohrlappen.
24 **dribbling:** sabbernd.

MAHON. Then the blight of the sacred drought upon
myself and him, for I never went mad to this day, and
I not three weeks with the Limerick girls drinking
myself silly and parlatic from the dusk to dawn. *(To
Widow Quin, suddenly.)* Is my visage astray?

WIDOW QUIN. It is then. You're a sniggering maniac, a
child could see.

MAHON *(getting up more cheerfully)*. Then I'd best be
going to the Union beyond, and there'll be a welcome
before me, I tell you *(with great pride)*, and I a
terrible and fearful case, the way that there I was one
time screeching in a straitened waistcoat with seven
doctors writing out my sayings in a printed book.
Would you believe that?

WIDOW QUIN. If you're a wonder itself, you'd best be
hasty, for them lads caught a maniac one time and
pelted the poor creature till he ran out raving and
foaming and was drowned in the sea.

MAHON *(with philosophy)*. It's true mankind is the divil
when your head's astray. Let me out now and I'll slip
down the boreen and not see them so.

WIDOW QUIN *(showing him out)*. That's it. Run to the
right, and not a one will see.
(He runs off.)

PHILLY *(wisely)*. You're at some gaming, Widow Quin;

---

1 **blight:** Brand(fäule), Pestluft.
4 **parlatic** (= *paralytic*): gelähmt.
5 **astray:** verzogen, entstellt; verwirrt (vgl. Z. 20).
6 **to snigger:** kichern.
9 **Union:** Abk. für *Union House:* Armenhaus.
12 **straitened waistcoat:** Zwangsjacke.
17 **to pelt:** bewerfen.
25 **You're at some gaming:** Sie führen etwas im Schilde.

but I'll walk after him and give him his dinner and a
time to rest, and I'll see then if he's raving or as sane
as you.

WIDOW QUIN *(annoyed)*. If you go near the lad, let you be
wary of your head, I'm saying. Didn't you hèar him
telling he was crazed at times?

PHILLY. I heard him telling a power; and I'm thinking
we'll have right sport, before night will fall. *(He goes
out.)*

JIMMY. Well, Philly's a conceited and foolish man. How
could that madman have his senses and his brain-pan
slit? I'll go after them and see him turn on Philly now.
*(He goes, Widow Quin hides poteen behind counter.
Then hubbub outside.)*

VOICES. There you are! Good jumper! Grand lepper!
Darlint boy! He's the racer! Bear him on, will you!
*(Christy comes in, in Jockey's dress, with Pegeen
Mike, Sara, and other girls, and men.)*

PEGEEN *(to Crowd)*. Go on now and don't destroy him
and he drenching with sweat. Go along, I'm saying,
and have your tug-of-warring till he's dried his
skin.

CROWD. Here's his prizes! A bagpipes! A fiddle was
played by a poet in the years gone by! A flat and

---

6 **crazed:** wahnsinnig, tobsüchtig.
10 **conceited:** eingebildet.
14 **hubbub:** Lärm, Getöse.
16 **darlint:** *darling.*
20 **to drench with sweat:** vor Schweiß triefen, schweißgebadet sein (*to
drench:* durchnässen).
21 **tug-of-warring:** Tauziehen.
23 **bagpipes** (pl.): Dudelsack.
   fiddle: Fiedel, Geige.

three-thorned blackthorn would lick the scholars out
of Dublin town!

CHRISTY (*taking prizes from the men*). Thank you kindly,
the lot of you. But you'd say it was little only I did this
day if you'd seen me a while since striking my one
single blow.

TOWN CRIER (*outside, ringing a bell*). Take notice, last
event of this day! Tug-of-warring on the green below!
Come on, the lot of you! Great achievements for all
Mayo men!

PEGEEN. Go on, and leave him for to rest and dry. Go
on, I tell you, for he'll do no more. (*She hustles
Crowd out; Widow Quin following them.*)

MEN (*going*). Come on then. Good luck for the while!

PEGEEN (*radiantly, wiping his face with her shawl*). Well
you're the lad, and you'll have great times from this
out when you could win that wealth of prizes, and you
sweating in the heat of noon!

CHRISTY (*looking at her with delight*). I'll have great
times if I win the crowning prize I'm seeking now,
and that's your promise that you'll wed me in a
fortnight, when our banns is called.

PEGEEN (*backing away from him*). You've right daring
to go ask me that, when all knows you'll be starting to
some girl in your own townland, when your father's
rotten in four months, or five.

CHRISTY (*indignantly*). Starting from you, is it? (*He

---

1 **blackthorn:** Schwarz-, Schlehdorn. Der Knotenstock gehört zur
typischen Ausstattung der Landbevölkerung.
  to lick: hier: prügeln.
22 **banns** (pl.): (Heirats-)Aufgebot.
25 **townland:** Bezirk, Distrikt.
27 **indignantly** (adv.): entrüstet.

follows her.) I will not then, and when the airs is
warming in four months or five, it's then yourself and
me should be pacing Neifin in the dews of night, the
times sweet smells do be rising, and you'd see a little
5   shiny new moon maybe sinking on the hills.

PEGEEN (*looking at him playfully*). And it's that kind of a
poacher's love you'd make, Christy Mahon, on the
sides of Neifin, when the night is down?

CHRISTY. It's little you'll think if my love's a poacher's
10   or an earl's itself when you'll feel my two hands
stretched around you, and I squeezing kisses on your
puckered lips till I'd feel a kind of pity for the Lord
God is all ages sitting lonesome in his golden chair.

PEGEEN. That'll be right fun, Christy Mahon, and any
15   girl would walk her heart out before she'd meet a
young man was your like for eloquence or talk at all.

CHRISTY (*encouraged*). Let you wait to hear me talking
till we're astray in Erris when Good Friday's by,
drinking a sup from a well, and making mighty kisses
20   with our wetted mouths, or gaming in a gap of
sunshine with yourself stretched back unto your neck-
lace in the flowers of the earth.

PEGEEN (*in a lower voice, moved by his tone*). I'd be nice
so, is it?

25   CHRISTY (*with rapture*). If the mitred bishops seen you
that time, they'd be the like of the holy prophets, I'm
thinking, do be straining the bars of Paradise to lay

---

7 **poacher:** Wilderer, Wilddieb.
11 **to squeeze:** drücken.
12 **puckered lips:** gespitzte, zusammengezogene Lippen.
16 **eloquence:** Beredtheit.
25 **mitred:** mit einer Mitra (*mitre:* Mitra, Bischofshut).
27 **to strain:** strecken, auseinanderdrücken.

eyes on the Lady Helen of Troy, and she abroad
pacing back and forward with a nosegay in her golden
shawl.

PEGEEN *(with real tenderness)*. And what is it I have,
Christy Mahon, to make me fitting entertainment for
the like of you that has such poet's talking, and such
bravery of heart?

CHRISTY *(in a low voice)*. Isn't there the light of seven
heavens in your heart alone, the way you'll be an
angel's lamp to me from this out, and I abroad in the
darkness spearing salmons in the Owen or the Car-
rowmore.

PEGEEN. If I was your wife, I'd be along with you those
nights, Christy Mahon, the way you'd see I was a
great hand at coaxing bailiffs, or coining funny nick-
names for the stars of night.

CHRISTY. You, is it! Taking your death in the hailstones
or the fogs of dawn.

PEGEEN. Yourself and me would shelter easy in a narrow
bush, *(with a qualm of dread)* but we're only talking
maybe, for this would be a poor thatched place to
hold a fine lad is the like of you.

CHRISTY *(putting his arm round her)*. If I wasn't a good
Christian, it's on my naked knees I'd be saying my
prayers and paters to every jackstraw you have roof-

---

2 **nosegay:** Blumenstrauß, Sträußchen.
4 **tenderness:** Zärtlichkeit, Zartheit.
11 **to spear:** durchbohren, aufspießen.
   salmon: Salm, Lachs.
15 f. **nickname:** Spitzname.
17 **hailstone:** Hagelkorn, Schloße.
19 **to shelter:** Unterschlupf, Schutz finden.
25 **pater:** Vaterunser.
   jackstraw: Strohhalm.

ing your head, and every stony pebble is paving the
laneway to your door.

PEGEEN (*radiantly*). If that's the truth, I'll be burning
candles from this out to the miracles of God have
5   brought you from the south to-day, and I with my
gowns bought ready the way that I can wed you, and
not wait at all.

CHRISTY. It's miracles and that's the truth. Me there
toiling a long while, and walking a long while, not
10   knowing at all I was drawing all times nearer to this
holy day.

PEGEEN. And myself a girl was tempted often to go
sailing the seas till I'd marry a Jew-man with ten kegs
of gold, and I not knowing at all there was the like of
15   you drawing nearer like the stars of God.

CHRISTY. And to think I'm long years hearing women
talking that talk to all bloody fools, and this the first
time I've heard the like of your voice talking sweetly
for my own delight.

20 PEGEEN. And to think it's me is talking sweetly, Christy
Mahon, and I the fright of seven townlands for my
biting tongue. Well the heart's a wonder, and I'm
thinking there won't be our like in Mayo for gallant
lovers from this hour to-day. (*Drunken singing is
25   heard outside.*) There's my father coming from the
wake, and when he's had his sleep we'll tell him, for
he's peaceful then: (*They separate.*)

MICHAEL (*singing outside*) –
       The jailor and the turnkey

---

13 **keg:** Fäßchen.
29 **jailor:** Kerkermeister.
    turnkey: Schließer.

They quickly ran us down,
And brought us back as prisoners
Once more to Cavan town.
(He comes in supported by Shawn.)
There we lay bewailing
All in a prison bound. . . .
*(He sees Christy. Goes and shakes him drunkenly by
the hand, while Pegeen and Shawn talk on the left.)*
MICHAEL *(to Christy)*. The blessing of God and the holy
angels on your head, young fellow. I hear tell you're
after winning all in the sports below; and wasn't it a
shame I didn't bear you along with me to Kate
Cassidy's wake, a fine, stout lad, the like of you, for
you'd never see the match of it for flows of drink, the
way when we sunk her bones at noonday in her
narrow grave, there were five men, aye, and six men,
stretched out retching speechless on the holy stones.
CHRISTY *(uneasily, watching Pegeen)*. Is that the truth?
MICHAEL. It is then, and aren't you a louty schemer to go
burying your poor father unbeknownst when you'd a
right to throw him on the crupper of a Kerry mule
and drive him westwards, like holy Joseph in the days
gone by, the way we could have given him a decent
burial and not have him rotting beyond and not a
Christian drinking a smart drop to the glory of his
soul.

1 **to run s.o. down:** jdn. einholen.
5 **to bewail:** (be)klagen.
12 **to bear s.o. along:** jdn. mitnehmen.
17 **to retch:** sich erbrechen.
19 **louty:** tölpelhaft.
20 **unbeknownst** (dial.): unbekannt.
21 **crupper:** Kruppe (Kreuz eines Pferdes).
25 **a smart drop:** ein scharfer, kräftiger Tropfen.

CHRISTY *(gruffly)*. It's well enough he's lying for the likes
of him.

MICHAEL *(slapping him on the back)*. Well, aren't you a
hardened slayer? It'll be a poor thing for the house-
5 hold man where you go sniffing for a female wife; and
(pointing to Shawn) look beyond at that shy and
decent Christian I have chosen for my daughter's
hand, and I after getting the gilded dispensation this
day for to wed them now.

10 CHRISTY. And you'll be wedding them this day, is it?

MICHAEL *(drawing himself up)*. Aye. Are you thinking,
if I'm drunk itself I'd leave my daughter living single
with a little frisky rascal is the like of you?

PEGEEN *(breaking away from Shawn)*. Is it the truth the
15 dispensation's come?

MICHAEL *(triumphantly)*. Father Reilly's after reading it
in gallous Latin, and "It's come in the nick of time,"
says he; "so I'll wed them in a hurry, dreading that
young gaffer who'd capsize the stars."

20 PEGEEN *(fiercely)*. He's missed his nick of time, for it's
that lad, Christy Mahon, that I'm wedding now.

MICHAEL *(loudly, with horror)*. You'd be making him a
son to me and he wet and crusted with his father's
blood?

25 PEGEEN. Aye. Wouldn't it be a bitter thing for a girl to

---

4 **slayer:** Totschläger, Mörder.
8 **gilded:** vergoldet.
13 **frisky:** ausgelassen, munter.
   rascal: Schelm.
17 **gallous:** schneidig, forsch.
   in the nick of time: im richtigen Augenblick.
19 **to capsize:** zum Kentern bringen, umkippen.

go marrying the like of Shaneen, and he a middling
kind of a scarecrow with no savagery or fine words in
him at all?

MICHAEL *(gasping and sinking on a chair)*. Oh, aren't
you a heathen daughter to go shaking the fat of my
heart, and I swamped and drownded with the weight
of drink? Would you have them turning on me the
way that I'd be roaring to the dawn of day with the
wind upon my heart? Have you not a word to aid me,
Shaneen? Are you not jealous at all?

SHAWN *(in great misery)*. I'd be afeard to be jealous of a
man did slay his da.

PEGEEN. Well, it'd be a poor thing to go marrying your
like. I'm seeing there's a world of peril for an orphan
girl, and isn't it a great blessing I didn't wed you,
before himself came walking from the west or south.

SHAWN. It's a queer story you'd go picking a dirty tramp
up from the highways of the world.

PEGEEN *(playfully)*. And you think you're a likely beau
to go straying along with, the shiny Sundays of the
opening year, when it's sooner on a bullock's liver
you'd put a poor girl thinking than on the lily or the
rose.

SHAWN. And have you no mind of my weight of passion,

---

2 **scarecrow:** Vogelscheuche.
6 **to be swamped:** überschwemmt, untergegangen sein.
   to be drownded (= *drowned*): versunken, ertrunken sein.
10 **jealous:** eifersüchtig.
14 **peril:** Gefahr.
17f. **to pick up:** auflesen.
19 **beau:** Verehrer.
20 **to stray along:** umherstreifen, wandern.
21 **bullock's liver:** Ochsenleber.

and the holy dispensation, and the drift of heifers I
am giving, and the golden ring?

PEGEEN. I'm thinking you're too fine for the like of me,
Shawn Keogh of Killakeen, and let you go off till
5 you'd find a radiant lady with droves of bullocks on
the plains of Meath, and herself bedizened in the
diamond jewelleries of Pharaoh's ma. That'd be your
match, Shaneen. So God save you now! *(She retreats
behind Christy.)*

10 SHAWN. Won't you hear me telling you. . . .

CHRISTY *(with ferocity)*. Take yourself from this, young
fellow, or I'll maybe add a murder to my deeds to-
day.

MICHAEL *(springing up with a shriek)*. Murder is it? Is it
15 mad yous are? Would you go making murder in this
place, and it piled with poteen for our drink to-night?
Go on to the foreshore if it's fighting you want, where
the rising tide will wash all traces from the memory of
man. *(Pushing Shawn towards Christy.)*

20 SHAWN *(shaking himself free, and getting behind Michael)*. I'll not fight him, Michael James. I'd liefer
live a bachelor simmering in passions to the end of
time, than face a lepping savage the like of him has
descended from the Lord knows where. Strike him

---

1 **drift:** Schar, Herde, Haufen.
  heifer: junge Kuh, Färse.
5 **drove:** Herde.
6 **to bedizen:** herausputzen, ausstaffieren.
11 **ferocity:** Wildheit, Grausamkeit.
17 **foreshore:** Strand, Klippen.
22 **bachelor:** Junggeselle.
  to simmer: sieden, wallen.
23 **savage:** Wilder, Rohling.

yourself, Michael James, or you'll lose my drift of
heifers and my blue bull from Sneem.

MICHAEL. Is it me fight him, when it's father-slaying he's
bred to now? *(Pushing Shawn.)* Go on you fool and
fight him now.

SHAWN *(coming forward a little)*. Will I strike him with
my hand?

MICHAEL. Take the loy is on your western side.

SHAWN. I'd be afeard of the gallows if I struck with that.

CHRISTY *(taking up the loy)*. Then I'll make you face the
gallows or quit off from this. *(Shawn flies out of the
door.)*

CHRISTY. Well, fine weather be after him, *(going to
Michael, coaxingly)* and I'm thinking you wouldn't
wish to have that quaking blackguard in your house at
all. Let you give us your blessing and hear her swear
her faith to me, for I'm mounted on the spring-tide of
the stars of luck the way it'll be good for any to have
me in the house.

PEGEEN *(at the other side of Michael)*. Bless us now, for I
swear to God I'll wed him, and I'll not renege.

MICHAEL *(standing up in the centre, holding on to both of
them)*. It's the will of God, I'm thinking, that all
should win an easy or a cruel end, and it's the will of
God that all should rear up lengthy families for the
nurture of the earth. What's a single man, I ask you,
eating a bit in one house and drinking a sup in

9 **gallows** (pl.): Galgen.
15 **to quake:** zittern, beben.
17 **spring-tide:** Springflut.
21 **to renege:** sein Wort brechen, widerrufen.
25 **lengthy families:** alte Familiengeschlechter.
26 **nurture:** Pflege, Wartung.

another, and he with no place of his own, like an
old braying jackass strayed upon the rocks? *(To
Christy.)* It's many would be in dread to bring your
like into their house for to end them maybe with a
5 sudden end; but I'm a decent man of Ireland, and I'd
liefer face the grave untimely and I seeing a score of
grandsons growing up little gallant swearers by the
name of God, than go peopling my bedside with puny
weeds the like of what you'd breed, I'm thinking, out
10 of Shaneen Keogh. *(He joins their hands.)* A daring
fellow is the jewel of the world, and a man did split
his father's middle with a single clout should have
the bravery of ten, so may God and Mary and St. Patrick bless you, and increase you from this mortal
15 day.

CHRISTY and PEGEEN. Amen, O Lord!

*(Hubbub outside. Old Mahon rushes in, followed by
all the crowd and Widow Quin. He makes a rush at
Christy, knocks him down, and begins to beat him.)*

20 PEGEEN *(dragging back his arm)*. Stop that, will you.
Who are you at all?

MAHON. His father, God forgive me!

PEGEEN *(drawing back)*. Is it rose from the dead?

MAHON. Do you think I look so easy quenched with the
25 tap of a loy? *(Beats Christy again.)*

---

2 **to bray:** iahen, trompeten.
   jackass: männlicher Esel; (fig.) Dummkopf.
6 **untimely:** vorzeitig.
8 **puny:** winzig, mickerig.
9 **weed:** schmächtiger Mensch, Schwächling.
20 **to drag back:** zurückziehen.
24 **to quench:** auslöschen.
25 **tap:** leichter Schlag.

PEGEEN *(glaring at Christy)*. And it's lies you told, letting
on you had him slitted, and you nothing at all.

CHRISTY *(catching Mahon's stick)*. He's not my father.
He's a raving maniac would scare the world. *(Point-*
5 *ing to Widow Quin.)* Herself knows it is true.

CROWD. You're fooling Pegeen! The Widow Quin seen
him this day and you likely knew! You're a liar!

CHRISTY *(dumbfounded)*. It's himself was a liar, lying
stretched out with an open head on him, letting on he
10 was dead.

MAHON. Weren't you off racing the hills before I got my
breath with the start I had seeing you turn on me at
all?

PEGEEN. And to think of the coaxing glory we had given
15 him, and he after doing nothing but hitting a soft
blow and chasing northward in a sweat of fear. Quit
off from this.

CHRISTY *(piteously)*. You've seen my doings this day,
and let you save me from the old man; for why would
20 you be in such a scorch of haste to spur me to destruction now?

PEGEEN. It's there your treachery is spurring me, till I'm
hard set to think you're the one I'm after lacing in
my heart-strings half-an-hour gone by. *(To Mahon.)*
25 Take him on from this, for I think bad the world

---

1 **to glare at s.o.:** jdn. anfunkeln.
8 **dumbfounded:** sprachlos, verblüfft.
12 **start:** Überraschung, Verblüffung.
16 **sweat of fear:** Angstschweiß.
20 **scorch of haste:** rasende Eile.
   to spur: antreiben, anspornen.
25 **to think bad:** bereuen, sich schämen (vgl. *to feel bad about s.th.* ›sich
   für etwas schämen‹).

should see me raging for a Munster liar and the fool
of men.

MAHON. Rise up now to retribution, and come on with
me.

5 CROWD (*jeeringly*). There's the playboy! There's the lad
thought he'd rule the roost in Mayo. Slate him now,
Mister.

CHRISTY (*getting up in shy terror*). What is it drives you
to torment me here, when I'd ask the thunders of the
10 might of God to blast me if I ever did hurt to any
saving only that one single blow.

MAHON (*loudly*). If you didn't, you're a poor good-for-
nothing, and isn't it by the like of you the sins of the
whole world are committed?

15 CHRISTY (*raising his hands*). In the name of the Almighty
God. . . .

MAHON. Leave troubling the Lord God. Would you have
him sending down droughts, and fevers, and the old
hen and the cholera morbus?

20 CHRISTY (*to Widow Quin*). Will you come between us
and protect me now?

WIDOW QUIN. I've tried a lot, God help me! and my share
is done.

CHRISTY (*looking round in desperation*). And I must go
25 back into my torment is it, or run off like a vagabond
straying through the Unions with the dusts of August
making mudstains in the gullet of my throat, or the

---

3 **retribution:** Vergeltung.
6 **roost:** Hühnerstall.
  to slate (ir.): prügeln, durchwalken.
10 **to blast:** in die Luft sprengen, vernichten.
18f. **the old hen** (fig.): Grippe.
19 **morbus** (lat.): Krankheit.
27 **mudstain:** Schmutzfleck.

winds of March blowing on me till I'd take an oath I
felt them making whistles of my ribs within.

SARA. Ask Pegeen to aid you. Her like does often
change.

CHRISTY. I will not then, for there's torment in the
splendour of her like and she a girl any moon of
midnight would take pride to meet, facing south-
wards on the heaths of Keel. But what did I want
crawling forward to scorch my understanding at her
flaming brow?

PEGEEN *(to Mahon, vehemently, fearing she will break
into tears)*. Take him on from this or I'll set the young
lads to destroy him here.

MAHON *(going to him, shaking his stick)*. Come on now if
you wouldn't have the company to see you skelped.

PEGEEN *(half laughing, through her tears)*. That's it, now
the world will see him pandied, and he an ugly liar
was playing off the hero and the fright of men!

CHRISTY *(to Mahon, very sharply)*. Leave me go!

CROWD. That's it. Now Christy. If them two set fighting,
it will lick the world.

MAHON *(making a grab at Christy)*. Come here to me.

CHRISTY *(more threateningly)*. Leave me go, I'm saying.

MAHON. I will maybe when your legs is limping, and your
back is blue.

CROWD. Keep it up, the two of you. I'll back the old one.
Now the playboy.

CHRISTY *(in low and intense voice)*. Shut your yelling, for

---

8 **heath:** Heide.
12 **to take s.o. on:** jdn. mitnehmen, wegholen.
17 **to pandy** (ir.): verhauen.
18 **to play off the hero:** den Helden spielen.
26 **Keep it up, the two of you:** Weiter so, ihr zwei!
28 **yelling:** (gellendes) Geschrei, Gebrüll.

if you're after making a mighty man of me this day by
the power of a lie, you're setting me now to think if
it's a poor thing to be lonesome, it's worse maybe go
mixing with the fools of earth.

5   *(Mahon makes a movement towards him.)*

CHRISTY *(almost shouting).* Keep off . . . lest I do show a
blow unto the lot of you would set the guardian
angels winking in the clouds above. *(He swings round
with a sudden rapid movement and picks up a loy.)*

10   CROWD *(half frightened, half amused).* He's going mad!
Mind yourselves! Run from the idiot!

CHRISTY. If I am an idiot, I'm after hearing my voice this
day saying words would raise the topknot on a poet in
a merchant's town. I've won your racing and your

15   lepping and . . .

MAHON. Shut your gullet and come on with me.

CHRISTY. I'm going but I'll stretch you first.

*(He runs at Old Mahon with the loy, chases him out of
the door, followed by Crowd and Widow Quin. There*

20   *is a great noise outside, then a yell, and dead silence
for a moment. Christy comes in, half dazed, and goes
to fire.)*

WIDOW QUIN *(coming in, hurriedly, and going to him).*
They're turning again you. Come on or you'll be

25   hanged indeed.

CHRISTY. I'm thinking from this out, Pegeen'll be giving
me praises the same as in the hours gone by.

---

6 **lest:** damit . . . nicht.
8 **to wink:** die Augen schließen.
13 **topknot:** Haarbüschel.
17 **to stretch s.o.:** jdn. zur Strecke bringen.
21 **dazed:** betäubt, verwirrt.

WIDOW QUIN *(impatiently)*. Come by the back-door. I'd
think bad to have you stifled on the gallows tree.

CHRISTY *(indignantly)*. I will not then. What good'd be
my life-time if I left Pegeen?

5 WIDOW QUIN. Come on and you'll be no worse than you
were last night; and you with a double murder this
time to be telling to the girls.

CHRISTY. I'll not leave Pegeen Mike.

WIDOW QUIN *(impatiently)*. Isn't there the match of her in
10 every parish public, from Binghamstown unto the
plain of Meath? Come on, I tell you, and I'll find you
finer sweethearts at each waning moon.

CHRISTY. It's Pegeen I'm seeking only, and what'd I care
if you brought me a drift of chosen females, standing
15 in their shifts itself maybe, from this place to the
Eastern World.

SARA *(runs in, pulling off one of her petticoats)*. They're
going to hang him. *(Holding out petticoat and shawl.)*
Fit these upon him and let him run off to the east.

20 WIDOW QUIN. He's raving now; but we'll fit them on him
and I'll take him in the ferry to the Achill boat.

CHRISTY *(struggling feebly)*. Leave me go, will you, when
I'm thinking of my luck to-day, for she will wed me
surely and I a proven hero in the end of all. *(They try
25 to fasten petticoat round him.)*

WIDOW QUIN. Take his left hand and we'll pull him now.
Come on, young fellow.

CHRISTY *(suddenly starting up)*. You'll be taking me

---

2 **to stifle:** ersticken, die Luft abdrücken.
12 **to wane:** abnehmen (Mond).
19 **to fit s.th. upon s.o.:** jdm. etwas anziehen.
21 **ferry:** Fährboot.

from her? You're jealous, is it, of her wedding me?
Go on from this. *(He snatches up a stool, and
threatens them with it.)*

WIDOW QUIN *(going)*. It's in the mad-house they should
put him not in jail at all. We'll go by the back-door to
call the doctor and we'll save him so.

*(She goes out, with Sara, through inner room. Men
crowd in the doorway. Christy sits down again by the
fire.)*

MICHAEL *(in a terrified whisper)*. Is the old lad killed
surely?

PHILLY. I'm after feeling the last gasps quitting his heart.
(They peer in at Christy.)

MICHAEL *(with a rope)*. Look at the way he is. Twist a
hangman's knot on it and slip it over his head while
he's not minding at all.

PHILLY. Let you take it, Shaneen. You're the soberest of
all that's here.

SHAWN. Is it me to go near him, and he the wickedest
and worst with me? Let you take it, Pegeen Mike.

PEGEEN. Come on, so. *(She goes forward with the others,
and they drop the double hitch over his head.)*

CHRISTY. What ails you?

SHAWN *(triumphantly, as they pull the rope tight on his
arms)*. Come on to the peelers till they stretch you
now.

CHRISTY. Me!

MICHAEL. If we took pity on you, the Lord God would
maybe bring us ruin from the law to-day, so you'd

---

15 **hangman:** Henker.
22 **hitch:** Knoten (in einem Seil).

best come easy, for hanging is an easy and a speedy
end.

CHRISTY. I'll not stir. *(To Pegeen.)* And what is it you'll
say to me and I after doing it this time in the face of
5   all?

PEGEEN. I'll say a strange man is a marvel with his
mighty talk; but what's a squabble in your back-yard
and the blow of a loy, have taught me that there's a
great gap between a gallous story and a dirty deed.
10   *(To men.)* Take him on from this, or the lot of us will
be likely put on trial for his deed to-day.

CHRISTY *(with horror in his voice)*. And it's yourself will
send me off to have a horny-fingered hangman hitch-
ing his bloody slip-knots at the butt of my ear?

15   MEN *(pulling rope)*. Come on, will you?
    (He is pulled down on the floor.)

CHRISTY *(twisting his legs round the table)*. Cut the rope,
Pegeen, and I'll quit the lot of you and live from this
out like the madmen of Keel, eating muck and green
20   weeds on the faces of the cliffs.

PEGEEN. And leave us to hang, is it, for a saucy liar, the
like of you? *(To men.)* Take him on out from this.

SHAWN. Pull a twist on his neck, and squeeze him so.

PHILLY. Twist yourself. Sure he cannot hurt you, if you
25   keep your distance from his teeth alone.

---

1 **easy:** hier: nachgiebig, gefügig.
7 **squabble:** Streit, Gezänk.
13 f. **to hitch:** festmachen.
14 **slip-knot:** Schlinge.
19 **muck:** Dung.
20 **weed:** Unkraut; Seetang.
21 **saucy:** unverschämt, frech.

SHAWN. I'm afeard of him. *(To Pegeen.)* Lift a lighted
  sod will you and scorch his leg.

PEGEEN *(blowing the fire with a bellows)*. Leave go now
  young fellow or I'll scorch your shins.

5 CHRISTY. You're blowing for to torture me? *(His voice
  rising and growing stronger.)* That's your kind, is it?
  Then let the lot of you be wary, for if I've to face the
  gallows I'll have a gay march down, I tell you, and
  shed the blood of some of you before I die.

10 SHAWN *(in terror)*. Keep a good hold, Philly. Be wary for
  the love of God, for I'm thinking he would liefest
  wreak his pains on me.

CHRISTY *(almost gaily)*. If I do lay my hands on you, it's
  the way you'll be at the fall of night hanging as a
15 scarecrow for the fowls of hell. Ah, you'll have a
  gallous jaunt I'm saying, coaching out through Limbo
  with my father's ghost.

SHAWN *(to Pegeen)*. Make haste, will you. Oh, isn't he a
  holy terror, and isn't it true for Father Reilly that all
20 drink's a curse that has the lot of you so shaky and
  uncertain now.

CHRISTY. If I can wring a neck among you, I'll have a
  royal judgment looking on the trembling jury in the
  courts of law. And won't there be crying out in Mayo
25 the day I'm stretched upon the rope with ladies

---

  1 **lighted:** hier: glühend.
  3 **bellows** (pl.): Blasebalg.
  4 **shin:** Schienbein.
 12 **to wreak:** rächen.
 15 **fowls** (pl.): Federvieh.
 16 **jaunt:** Ausflug, Spaziergang.
    to coach: kutschieren.
    limbo: Vorhölle.

in their silks and satins snivelling in their lacy ker-
chiefs, and they rhyming songs and ballads on the
terror of my fate? *(He squirms round on the floor
and bites Shawn's leg.)*

5 SHAWN *(shrieking)*. My leg's bit on me! He's the like of a
mad dog, I'm thinking, the way that I will surely die.

CHRISTY *(delighted with himself)*. You will then, the way
you can shake out hell's flags of welcome for my
coming in two weeks or three, for I'm thinking Satan

10 hasn't many have killed their da in Kerry and in Mayo
too.

*(Old Mahon comes in behind on all fours and looks
on unnoticed.)*

MEN *(to Pegeen)*. Bring the sod, will you.

15 PEGEEN *(coming over)*. God help him so. *(Burns his leg.)*

CHRISTY *(kicking and screaming)*. Oh, glory be to God!
*(He kicks loose from the table, and they all drag him
towards the door.)*

JIMMY *(seeing Old Mahon)*. Will you look what's come

20 in?
(They all drop Christy and run left.)

CHRISTY *(scrambling on his knees face to face with Old
Mahon)*. Are you coming to be killed a third time or
what ails you now?

25 MAHON. For what is it they have you tied?

CHRISTY. They're taking me to the peelers to have me
hanged for slaying you.

---

1 **in silks and satins** (pl.): etwa: in Samt und Seide.
   to snivel: schniefen, schluchzen.
   lacy: spitzenbesetzt.
3 **to squirm round:** sich herumdrehen, -winden.
22 **to scramble:** kriechen.
25 **to tie:** binden, fesseln.

MICHAEL *(apologetically)*. It is the will of God that all
should guard their little cabins from the treachery of
law and what would my daughter be doing if I was
ruined or was hanged itself?

5 MAHON *(grimly, loosening Christy)*. It's little I care if
you put a bag on her back and went picking cockles
till the hour of death; but my son and myself will be
going our own way and we'll have great times from
this out telling stories of the villainy of Mayo and the

10 fools is here. *(To Christy, who is freed.)* Come on
now.

CHRISTY. Go with you, is it! I will then, like a gallant
captain with his heathen slave. Go on now and I'll see
you from this day stewing my oatmeal and washing

15 my spuds, for I'm master of all fights from now.
(Pushing Mahon.) Go on, I'm saying.

MAHON. Is it me?

CHRISTY. Not a word out of you. Go on from this.

MAHON *(walking out and looking back at Christy over his*

20 *shoulder)*. Glory be to God! *(With a broad smile.)* I
am crazy again! *(Goes.)*

CHRISTY. Ten thousand blessings upon all that's here, for
you've turned me a likely gaffer in the end of all, the
way I'll go romancing through a romping lifetime

25 from this hour to the dawning of the judgment day.
(He goes out.)

MICHAEL. By the will of God, we'll have peace now for
our drinks. Will you draw the porter, Pegeen?

SHAWN *(going up to her)*. It's a miracle Father Reilly can

---

6 **cockle:** Herzmuschel.
14 **to stew:** kochen.

wed us in the end of all, and we'll have none to
trouble us when his vicious bite is healed.
PEGEEN *(hitting him a box on the ear).* Quit my sight.
*(Putting her shawl over her head and breaking out into
wild lamentations.)* Oh, my grief, I've lost him surely.
I've lost the only playboy of the western world.

CURTAIN

---

2 **vicious:** schlimm, böse.
3 **to hit s.o. a box on the ear:** jdm. eine Ohrfeige geben.

Editorische Notiz

Der englische Text folgt der Ausgabe: John Millington Synge, *Collected Works*, hrsg. von Robin Skelton, Bd. 4: *Plays II*, hrsg. von Ann Saddlemeyer, London: Oxford University Press, 1968. Das Glossar erklärt in der Regel alle Wörter, die über die Wertigkeitsstufe 4 des *Englischen Arbeitswörterbuchs* von Alfred Haase (Frankfurt a. M.: Moritz Diesterweg, ⁷1979) hinausgehen. Im Zweifelsfall wurde großzügig verfahren, d. h. eher eine Vokabel mehr aufgenommen als dort vorgesehen.

Eigenarten des irischen Englisch, die für Synge von besonderer Bedeutung sind:

I. Morphologie

1. *Ausgleich von Einzahl und Mehrzahl beim Verb*

   The peelers in this place is [= are] decent, droughty poor fellows (S. 26 f.).
   Sara Tansey, Susan Brady, Honor Blake! What in glory has you [= are you doing] here at this hour of day? (S. 45.)

2. *»Yous« als Mehrzahl des Fürworts »you«*

   Is it mad yous are? (S. 88.)

3. *Verwendung des Reflexivums zu Zwecken der Emphase*

   Herself [= she] knows it is true (S. 91).
   You're safe so with ourselves [= us] (S. 55).

4. *Häufiger Wegfall des Relativpronomens*

   There's the lad thought he'd rule the roost in Mayo (S. 92).
   Take the loy is on your western side (S. 89).

5. *Wegfall des indirekten Fragepronomens*

   Look now, is he roaring [= if he is roaring] (S. 35).

6. *Verwendung des Pertinenzdativs*

   My leg's bit on me! (S. 99.)
   An ugly young streeler with a murderous gob on him
   (S. 61).

7. *Adjektiv in der Funktion des Adverbs*

   You should have vexed him fearful [= fearfully] to make
   him strike (S. 62).
   Let you step off nimble [= nimbly] this time when there's
   none (S. 28).

8. *»let« + Pronomen + Verb als Befehlsform*

   Let you tell us your story (S. 46).
   Let you take it, Shaneen (S. 96).

9. *»will/would« statt »shall/should«*

   What name will we call you (S. 27).
   Will I strike him with my hand? (S. 89).

10. *Gehäufte Verwendung von konditionalem und konjunktivi-*
    schem »should« statt des Indikativs

    A lad would kill his father, I'm thinking, would face a foxy
    divil (S. 25).
    Well, you should have been a queer lot (S. 33).

II. Syntax

1. *Überaus häufige Umschreibung vom Typ »it is [. . . that]«*
   zu Zwecken der Emphase

   It was the girls were giving you heed: Die Mädchen freilich
   haben dich beachtet (S. 31).
   Is it mad yous are?: Seid ihr verrückt? (S. 88.)

2. *Häufige Verwischung des Unterschieds zwischen der ein-*
   fachen und der progressiven Verbform

   Go on, I'm saying [= say], and don't be waking [= wake]
   this place with your noise (S. 28).
   He's come up, I'm thinking [= think], stealing your hens
   (S. 18).

3. *Umschreibung mit »to do« + »be« + Partizip Präsens zum*
   Ausdruck einer wiederholten oder gewohnheitsmäßigen
   Handlung

   The clumsy young fellows do be plowing all times in the
   earth and dung (S. 42).
   There's harvest hundreds do be passing these days for the
   Sligo boat (S. 61 f.).

4. *»to be after« + Gerundium (+ Objekt) zum Ausdruck einer*
   kürzlich abgeschlossenen Handlung

   I'm after feeling [= I've just felt] the last gasps quitting his
   heart (S. 96).
   What's that she's after saying [= she's just said]? (S. 39.)

5. *Überaus häufige Verwendung der Konjunktion »and« als*
   Mittel loser Satzverbindung und in wechselnder Bedeutung

   You should have a thin stomach on you and you that
   length walking the world (S. 44).
   With that the sun came out between the cloud and the hill,
   and it shining green in my face (S. 48).
   Don't be talking, and we fooled to-day (S. 43).

Im Glossar verwendete Abkürzungen

adv.	adverb
arch.	archaic (veraltet)
dial.	dialectal (mundartlich)
fig.	figuratively (übertragen)
infml.	informal (umgangssprachlich)
ir.	irisch
lat.	lateinisch
o.s.	oneself
pl.	plural
s.o.	someone
s.th.	something

Literaturhinweise

I. *Ausgaben der Werke und Briefe, Übersetzungen*

John Millington Synge, *Collected Works*, hrsg. von R. Skelton, 4 Bde., London 1962–68; Bd. 1, *Poems*, hrsg. von R. Skelton, London 1962; Bd. 2, *Prose*, hrsg. von A. Price, London 1966; Bd. 3, *Plays I*, hrsg. von A. Saddlemyer, London 1968; Bd. 4, *Plays II*, hrsg. von A. Saddlemyer, London 1968.

John Millington Synge, *Plays, Poems, and Prose*, London 1941 (Everyman's Library, Bd. 968), Nachdr. London 1961 [u. ö.].

The Plays and Poems of J. M. Synge, hrsg. von T. R. Henn, London 1963.

John Millington Synge, *The Playboy of the Western World*, in: *Classic Irish Drama*, mit einer Einl. von W. A. Armstrong, Harmondsworth 1964 (Penguin Plays), S. 69–134.

John Millington Synge, *4 Plays*, hrsg. von R. Skelton, Oxford 1978 (World's Classics, Bd. 620).

John Millington Synge, *The Playboy of the Western World*, hrsg. von T. R. Henn, London 1961 (Methuen Theatre Classics).

John Millington Synge, *The Playboy of the Western World*, hrsg. von M. Kelsall, London 1985 (New Mermaids).

The Collected Letters of John Millington Synge, hrsg. von A. Saddlemyer, 2 Bde., Oxford 1983–84.

John Millington Synge, *Ein wahrer Held*, übers. von H. und A. Böll, in: *Theatrum Mundi: Englische und irische Dramen*, Frankfurt 1960.

John Millington Synge, *Der Held der westlichen Welt und andere Stücke*, übers. von P. Hacks, Frankfurt 1967 (Bibliothek Suhrkamp, Bd. 195).

II. *Bibliographien, Biographien, Nachschlagewerke*

Levitt, P., *J. M. Synge. A Bibliography of Published Criticism*, Dublin 1974.

Mikhail, E. H., *J. M. Synge. A Bibliography of Criticism*, London 1975.

Thornton, W., »J. M. Synge«, in: *Anglo-Irish Literature. A Review of Research*, hrsg. von R. J. Finneran, New York 1976, S. 315–365.

Greene, D. H. / Stephens, E. M., *J. M. Synge, 1871–1909*, New York 1959.

Bliss, A., »The Language of Synge«, in: *J. M. Synge. Centenary Papers 1971*, hrsg. von M. Harmon, Dublin 1972, S. 35–62.

Deane, S., »Synge's Poetic Use of Language«, in: *Mosaic 5* (1971) S. 27–36.

Joyce, P. W., *English as We Speak It in Ireland*, Dublin 1910.

Kiberd, D., *Synge and the Irish Language*, London 1979.

Kopper, E. A., *John Millington Synge. A Reference Guide*, London 1979.

Price, A. (Hrsg.), »*Riders to the Sea« and »The Playboy of the Western World*«, Oxford 1969 (Notes on English Literature, Bd. 31).

van Hamel, A. G., »On Anglo-Irish Syntax«, in: *Englische Studien* 45 (1912) S. 272–292.

III. *Sekundärliteratur*

a) Monographien und Sammelbände

Bushrui, S. B. (Hrsg.), *Sunshine and the Moon's Delight. A Centenary Tribute to John Millington Synge 1871–1909*, Gerrards Cross 1972.

Carpenter, A. (Hrsg.), *Place, Personality and the Irish Writer*, Smythe 1977.

Grene, N., *Synge. A Critical Study of the Plays*, London 1975.

Harmon, M. (Hrsg.), *J. M. Synge. Centenary Papers 1971*, Dublin 1972.

Johnson, T. O., *Synge: The Medieval and the Grotesque*, Gerrards Cross 1982.

Price, A., *Synge and Anglo-Irish Drama*, London 1961.

Ronsley, J. (Hrsg.), *Myth and Reality in Irish Literature*, Waterloo (Ontario) 1977.

Skelton, R., *The Writings of J. M. Synge*, New York 1971.

Thornton, W., *John Millington Synge and the Western Mind*, New York 1979.

Whitaker, T. R. (Hrsg.), *Twentieth Century Interpretations of »The Playboy of the Western World«*, Englewood Cliffs 1969.

b) Aufsätze

Bergner, H., »Synge. *The Playboy of the Western World*«, in: D. Mehl (Hrsg.), *Das englische Drama*, Bd. 2, Düsseldorf 1970, S. 202–216.

Breuer, H., »Männlichkeit in Synges *The Playboy of the Western World*«, in: *Germanisch-Romanische Monatsschrift* 32 (1982) S. 300–314.

Erzgräber, W., »John Millington Synge: *The Playboy of the Western World*«, in: H. Oppel (Hrsg.), *Das moderne englische Drama*, Berlin 1963, S. 91–106.

Habicht, W., »John Millington Synge«, in: *Englische Dichter der Moderne. Ihr Leben und Werk*, hrsg. von R. Sühnel und D. Riesner, Berlin 1971, S. 180–192.

Hirsch, E., »The Gallous Story and the Dirty Deed. The Two Playboys«, in: *Modern Drama* 26 (1983) S. 85–102.

Lengeler, R., »Phantasie und Komik in Synges *The Playboy of the Western World*«, in: *Germanisch-Romanische Monatsschrift* 19 (1969) S. 291–304.

Saddlemyer, A., »›A Share in the Dignity of the World‹: John Millington Synge's Aesthetic Theory«, in: R. Skelton / A. Saddlemyer (Hrsg.), *The World of W. B. Yeats*, Dub-

lin/Seattle 1965, S. 241–253; erw. Neuaufl. Seattle 1967, S. 207–219.
– »Synge and the Doors of Perception«, in: A. Carpenter (Hrsg.), *Place, Personality and the Irish Writer*, Smythe 1977, S. 97–120.

Nachwort

Leben und geschichtlicher Hintergrund

Die Haß-Liebe zu seiner Mutter und zu Irland sind zwei der Komponenten im Leben von John Millington Synge (1871 bis 1909), die seinen Werdegang als Schriftsteller und die Eigenart seiner Dramen grundlegend mitgeprägt haben.

Synges Eltern entstammten der protestantischen anglo-irischen Oberschicht; die Familie des Vaters John Hatch Synge war im 17. Jahrhundert aus England nach Irland eingewandert und im 18. zu Ansehen und zu Landbesitz gekommen, der freilich im Verlauf des 19. Jahrhunderts auf wenige Ländereien in Galway zusammengeschmolzen war. John Hatch Synge war Anwalt in Dublin und starb bereits ein Jahr nach der Geburt seines jüngsten Sohnes John Millington, der am 16. April 1871 in Rathfarnham, einem heutigen Vorort Dublins, auf die Welt kam. Nach dem Tod des Vaters lag die Erziehung der fünf Kinder ausschließlich in den Händen der Mutter Kathleen, geb. Traill, die die Tochter eines von Ulster nach Cork verschlagenen Katholikenfressers war und dessen evangelikalische Anschauungen auch auf ihre Umgebung ausstrahlte. Aus Synges halbautobiographischer Schrift »My Youth« wissen wir, daß bereits der sensible Junge gegen die grimmige evangelikalische Sündenlehre und das religiöse Eifertum seiner Mutter heimlich aufbegehrte. Der Halbwüchsige rebellierte dann vollends und verwarf unter dem Einfluß von Darwin alle Formen der Religion ein für allemal. Anlaß zu Spannungen in der Familie gaben nicht minder die politischen Ereignisse, etwa der Boykott, zu dem Parnell und die Landliga die zahlungsunwilligen und zahlungsunfähigen Pächter gegen die Landbesitzer ab 1880 aufriefen. Als Antwort auf den Boykott ließen die Gutsbesitzer die irischen Pächter durch ihre Verwalter (»agents«) und deren gewalttätige Helfershelfer (»emergency men«) vertreiben. Ein solcher Verwalter, im Westen und Osten des Landes für seine Vertreibungsmethoden berüchtigt, war auch Synges zweiter Bruder Edward. Während John von den Praktiken seines Bruders angewidert war, führte die Mutter gleich politische und religiöse Gründe ins Feld, um die Vertreibungen zu rechtfertigen und beharrte auf der Frage: »What would become of us if our tenants in Galway stopped paying their rents?« Freilich, wenn das Verhältnis zwischen Mutter und Sohn auch zeitlebens voller Spannungen blieb, so ist es doch nie zu einem gänzlichen Bruch gekommen. Ja, zum Tod seiner Mutter, kurz vor seinem eigenen Ende, schreibt Synge in einem Brief: »I cannot tell you how unspeakably sacred her memory seems to me. There is nothing in the world better or nobler than a single-hearted wife and mother.« Angesichts eines solchen Hin- und Hergerissenseins ist es kein Wunder, daß der Mensch Synge schwierig war und Züge einer Neurose verriet. Aus einer Narkose erwacht, schrie er plötzlich: »Damn the bloody Anglo-Saxon language that a man can't swear in without being vulgar!« Ein solcher Ausbruch läßt ahnen, daß die fortwährenden Bibelsprüche der Mutter und die Verteufelung der Gefühle als vulgär nicht ohne Wirkungen geblieben sind.

Wegen seiner Kränklichkeit hat der Junge bis zum Beginn seiner Universitätsstudien am Trinity College in Dublin nie für längere Zeit die Schule besucht, sondern erhielt dreimal wöchentlich den Besuch eines Privatlehrers. Innerlich einsam, entdeckte er früh seine Liebe zur Musik und nahm vom sechzehnten Jahr an Unterricht in Geige und Harmonielehre. Dieses Interesse für die Musik verstärkte sich noch in den folgenden Jahren und führte dazu, daß der Student seine Freizeitstudien an der Musikakademie mit größerem Ernst als sein Hauptstudium am Trinity College betrieb. Das Universitäts- und Studentenleben scheint den jungen Synge nicht sonderlich berührt zu haben. Die Lehrveranstaltungen beschränkte er auf ein Minimum und im Unterschied zur Musikakademie, wo er an den Orchesterproben regen Anteil nahm, scheint er auch keine engeren Beziehungen zu Mitstudenten oder Lehrern an der Universität geknüpft zu haben.

Auf die Studienjahre gehen allerdings auch Synges dichterische Anfänge zurück, die den Einfluß von Wordsworth verraten. Wordsworth hatte ja das einfache Volk zum Gegenstand seiner lyrischen Balladen gemacht und sich unter den englischen Romantikern am nachhaltigsten für eine Erneuerung der Dichtung aus dem Geist des Volkes eingesetzt. Und so ist es wohl kein Zufall, daß Synge, der an der Universität begonnen hatte, die irische Sprache und Geschichte zu studieren, sich zeitweilig (wie Yeats auch) für die Balladenimitationen des 19. Jahrhunderts begeisterte.

Auf dem Hintergrund dieser Anschauungen über die Bedeutung des Volkes für eine ursprüngliche Dichtung ist auch Yeats' Rat zu verstehen, den er Synge bei ihrem ersten Zusammentreffen in Paris 1896 gab: »Go to the Aran Islands. Live there as if you were one of the people themselves; express a life that has never found expression.« Synge befolgte den Rat und nutzte die Sommer der Jahre 1898–1902 für fünf Aufenthalte auf den Inseln und ergänzte so seine Lehrjahre auf dem Kontinent, in Deutschland, in Italien und vor allem in Paris. Die Aufenthalte auf den Aran-Inseln brachten nach Jahren des Stillstands endlich den erhofften dichterischen Durchbruch. Gleichermaßen unzufrieden mit den Symbolisten und Naturalisten, war es Synge in Paris dennoch nicht gelungen, seine Vorstellungen von einer in der Einbildungskraft des Volkes verwurzelten Dichtung zu verwirklichen. In den Bräuchen, Anschauungen und Erzählungen der Inselbewohner dagegen sah er noch so etwas wie Reste einer volkstümlichen Einbildungskraft am Werk. Synge war weder der erste, der die Möglichkeiten des irischen Englisch für die Dichtung genutzt hat, noch läßt sich seine »Kunstsprache« einseitig auf das Idiom der Aran-Inseln zurückführen. Im Vorwort zum *Playboy* erwähnt er selbst zusätzlich seine Ferienaufenthalte in Wicklow im Osten und die Sprache der Fischer und Hirten von Kerry bis Mayo im Westen des Landes. Den Aufenthalten auf den Aran-Inseln ist es jedoch offenbar zu verdanken, daß Synge seinen Gegenstand, die Darstellung des ländlichen Irland, endgültig fand und sich jetzt in der Lage sah, das irische Englisch so zu stilisieren, daß es seinen Vorstellungen einer ursprünglichen und volksnahen Dichtung möglichst nahekam. Jedenfalls tauchen in den Reisebildern *The Aran Islands* (1902) erstmalig die sprachlichen Eigenarten auf, die den ab 1903 erscheinenden Stücken *Riders to the Sea*, *In the Shadow of the Glen*, *The Well of the Saints*, *The Playboy of the Western World*, *The Tinker's Wedding*, *Deirdre* so unverwechselbar das Gepräge geben.

Die Uraufführung des *Playboy* im Abbey Theatre im Januar 1907 zog einen der größten Theaterskandale unseres Jahrhunderts nach sich. Nachdem es gegen Ende des ersten Abends zu Tumulten gekommen war, blieb keine der Aufführungen der folgenden Woche von Krawallen verschont. Regelmäßig nahm die Polizei Unruhestifter fest, die anderntags von einem Richter abgeurteilt wurden, der das Stück nicht kannte und darauf bestand, daß die Angeklagten und die Polizisten über Einzelheiten daraus berichteten. Hitzig ging es für eine Weile auch in der Presse und in öffentlichen Diskussionen zwischen den Kritikern aus dem Lager der Nationalisten und den Verteidigern mit Yeats an der Spitze zu. Bei der Wiederaufnahme des Stücks 1909, als Synge bereits zwei Monate tot war, flackerten die Streitereien erneut auf. Und als die Abbey-Theatre-Truppe 1911–12 eine Gastreise in die Vereinigten Staaten unternahm, gingen auch dort irischstämmige Nationalisten auf die Straße und veranlaßten zum Beispiel in Philadelphia, daß die ganze Truppe unter dem Vorwand, öffentliches Ärgernis zu erregen, für kurze Zeit festgenommen wurde. Inzwischen haben sich jedoch die Gemüter beruhigt und hüben wie drüben gilt der *Playboy* als ein Klassiker des Welttheaters.

Was Synges Verhältnis zu seinen Landsleuten betraf, so hätte er den Zusammenstoß mit den Nationalisten eigentlich voraussehen können. Er wußte, wie schwer sich viele Iren taten, einem unidealischen Bild des Nationalcharakters zu begegnen. »The crimeless virtuous side of Irish life is well known and cannot be disputed. The wilder – the Rabelaisian side of the Irish temperament is so wild it cannot be dealt with in book or periodical that is intended for Irish readers« (*Collected Works*, Bd. 2, S. XXV). Noch weniger als Yeats und Lady Gregory, mit denen zusammen er seit 1905 das Abbey Theatre leitete, war Synge jedoch bereit, einem blinden Nationalismus zuliebe Abstriche an seinen künstlerischen Idealen zuzulassen, ein geschöntes Abbild anstelle »der ganzen Lebenswirklichkeit« auf die Bühne zu bringen.

So war das Mißverständnis im Fall des *Playboy* fast unvermeidbar, denn Synges Gegenstand, der irische Westen, war nicht irgendein Gegenstand. Im Zuge der Erneuerungsbestrebungen des 19. Jahrhunderts war gerade der Bevölkerung des ländlichen Westens, die ja noch zum Teil die alte Sprache sprach, eine besondere Symbolrolle zugefallen. Hinter dem idealischen Klischee vom ausgebeuteten, aber edlen und grundehrlichen irischen Bauern stand die Erwartung einer ganzen gedemütigten Nation auf Erneuerung.

Statt aber dieser Idealisierung Vorschub zu leisten, stellte Synge im *Playboy* – so ein Zeitungskritiker – Irland als ein Land hin, »das von einer Horde mörderischer Wilder« bewohnt werde. Hinzu kam, daß Synge in den Augen der Nationalisten kein unbeschriebenes Blatt war. Wie Yeats und Lady Gregory entstammte er der englischstämmigen protestantischen Oberschicht; mehr noch als in Yeats' *Countess Cathleen* (1899), die in den Verdacht der Ketzerei geraten war, sahen Klerikale und Nationalisten in Synges frühem Stück *In the Shadow of the Glen* (1904) auch noch eine Befleckung der nationalen Ehre. Gegenüber der Verherrlichung des Vatermords im *Playboy* nahm sich freilich die Verherrlichung des Ehebruchs in dem früheren Stück noch harmlos aus. Statt die irischen Bauern zu verherrlichen, schien Synge sie im *Playboy* regelrecht zu verhöhnen. Da halfen ihm seine Beteuerungen auch nichts, daß er den Stoff einer wahren Begebenheit entnommen und daß er fast alle Wörter, an denen seine Kritiker jetzt Anstoß nahmen, selber irgendwann im Land gehört habe. Im Gegenteil, solche Beglaubigungen verleiteten viele erst recht dazu, an einen platten Realismus zu glauben und die Intention des Werks, seine innere Form gründlich mißzuverstehen.

Stoff, Handlung und Figuren

In einem ungedruckten Aufsatz »On Literary and Popular Poetry« hat Synge die Abhängigkeit der Autoren seiner Generation vom Volksgeist so charakterisiert: »The new poets did not copy the productions of the peasant but seized by instinct his inner mode of work.« Um diese innere Form des *Playboy* soll es im folgenden gehen, wobei wir nicht bei der Herkunft von Stoff, Figuren und Sprachelementen stehenbleiben wollen, sondern damit rechnen, daß Synge ihm charakteristisch erscheinende Züge aus diesen Elementen herausdestilliert und möglicherweise auch überzeichnet hat, um sie zu einem neuen Ganzen zu verschmelzen.

Mehrfach hat Synge betont, daß er seinen Stoff, den Vatermord, der ungesühnt bleibt, nicht frei erfunden, sondern einem wirklichen Vorfall nachgebildet hat. Und in *The Aran Islands* schreibt er, daß der älteste Bewohner von Inishmaan »often tells me about a Connaught man who killed his father with the blow of a spade when he was in passion, and then fled to this island and threw himself on the mercy of some of the natives with whom he was said to be related« (*Collected Works*, Bd. 2, S. 95).

Dieser Impuls, den Verbrecher zu schützen, so fährt Synge fort, sei im Westen Irlands weit verbreitet. Er erkennt darin eine Einstellung, die wohl auch mit dem Haß auf die Rechtsprechung der englischen Besatzer zusammenhänge, die aber zutiefst auf der Überzeugung beruhe, daß die Menschen keine Verbrecher seien, aber natürlich unter dem Einfluß von Leidenschaften zu Untaten fähig werden könnten. Jedoch sei später angesichts der Reue des Missetäters eine rechtskräftige Verurteilung und Bestrafung sinnlos.

Berücksichtigt man zusätzlich, daß der *Playboy* nicht aus einem Guß entstanden ist, sondern erhebliche Umwandlungen bis zur Endfassung durchgemacht hat, so erscheint zweierlei für die innere Form von Bedeutung. Synge sah erstens in der Abneigung der bäuerischen Bevölkerung gegen das offizielle Rechtswesen und in ihrem Verständnis des Verbrechens als einer Affekthandlung ein Zeichen für Ursprünglichkeit, was immer das letzten Endes sein mag. Und er erkannte zweitens schon sehr früh die komischen Möglichkeiten des Stoffes, also etwa den Eindruck der Verkehrung, den das Verhalten der Westler dem Verbrechen gegenüber auf Außenstehende machen mußte oder auch die herabgesetzte Urteilsfähigkeit und die Täuschungen, denen Affekttäter im besonderen unterworfen sind. Beides, die Suspendierung der üblichen moralischen und rationalen Sehweisen und die komische Verkehrung, wird uns deshalb auch bei der Besprechung von Handlung, Figuren und Sprachgebung wieder begegnen.

Zum Handlungsverlauf: Die Ausgangshandlung wird durch das Warten des ungleichen Brautpaars Pegeen und Shawn auf den kirchlichen Dispens gekennzeichnet, der die Verbindung der Wirtstochter mit ihrem Halbvetter ermöglichen soll, der freilich Pegeens Wunsch nach einem wirklichen Mann trotz aller seiner Böcke und Ländereien doch so wenig zu erfüllen verspricht. In der Nebenhandlung entspricht diesem zwiespältigen Warten die Bedrohung eines Besäufnisses; denn da Pegeen sich weigert, die Nacht über allein zu bleiben und Shawn aus Angst vor Father Reilly ihr nicht beistehen kann, können Pegeens Vater und seine Kumpane nicht zur Totenwache, wie es der Brauch erfordert. In diese Ungewißheit hinein platzt die Ankunft des Helden Christy Mahon, der sich sein Verbrechen, den Vatermord, von den zunächst grenzenlos neugierigen und dann restlos hingerissenen Dörflern entlocken läßt und die Stelle als Ausschankjunge im Wirtshaus annimmt. Damit steht der Feier der Totenwache nichts mehr im Wege, aber jetzt erscheint in der Haupthandlung die Heirat bedroht: Pegeen verjagt erst den ungeliebten Shawn und verteidigt ihre Beute auch gegen die Witwe Quin, die als Konkurrentin erschienen ist und am Ende des 1. Aktes unverrichteterdinge wieder abziehen muß. Das Gerangel um den Playboy zwischen Pegeen und der Witwe wiederholt und steigert sich im 2. Akt, wobei der Höhepunkt und die Wende mit dem unerwarteten Auftauchen von Christys totgeglaubtem Vater erreicht ist, just in dem Augenblick, in dem Christy sich endgültig von der

Witwe lossagen will. Alles, was jetzt noch folgt, Christys Pakt mit der listigen Witwe, um diese zum Schweigen zu bringen, seine Erfolge bei den Wettkämpfen und auch noch Christys erfolgreiche Werbung um Pegeens Liebe, zögert nur den Zeitpunkt hinaus, an dem der Playboy auch für Pegeen und die Dörfler durch das erneute Auftreten des Vaters seinen Nimbus als Vatermörder verliert. Dies geschieht im 3. Akt gerade dann, wenn der Wirt widerwillig der Heirat seiner Tochter mit dem angeblichen Vatermörder Christy zugestimmt hat und seinen unvergleichlichen Brautsegen spricht. Maßlos enttäuscht, verstößt Pegeen den Betrüger, während die schadenfrohe Menge sich auf das Schauspiel eines von seinem Vater geprügelten Schuljungen spitzt. Allerdings kommt es hier zu einem letzten Umschlag vor der Lösung des Konflikts: statt sich von seinem Vater abführen zu lassen, ergreift Christy plötzlich eine Hacke, mit der er seinen Vater verfolgt und hinter der Bühne, für jedermann unüberhörbar, niederschlägt. Wenn er aber geglaubt hat, auf diese Weise seinen Ruf als Vatermörder wieder herstellen zu können, so hat er sich abermals getäuscht. Denn die Dörfler fürchten nun, als Komplizen vor Gericht gestellt zu werden. Außerdem ist ihnen jetzt, in den Worten Pegeens, der Unterschied zwischen einer schneidigen Geschichte und einer schmutzigen Tat bewußt geworden. Am Schluß trennen sich die Wege erneut: während der Playboy mit seinem nicht totzukriegenden Vater in die ungebundene Welt der Landstreicher zieht, muß Pegeen ihren ungeliebten Shawn jetzt heiraten, zumal die kirchliche Erlaubnis inzwischen eingetroffen ist.

Wie beim Handlungsaufbau läßt sich auch hinter Synges Figuren der Einfluß der traditionellen Komödie ausmachen. So gibt es den bekannten Generationenkonflikt zwischen Christy und seinem Vater, zwischen Pegeen und der Witwe Quin. Wenn wir Christys eigener Darstellung glauben können, so ist es zum Streit gekommen, weil der Alte ihn mit einer abgrundhäßlichen Vettel verkuppeln wollte, um an deren Besitz zu kommen. Züge der liebestollen Alten weist auch die Witwe Quin auf, die sich aber noch stärker als Intrigantin erweist.

Christy selber und (auf seine Weise) auch der alte Mahon können als Ausprägungen des Alazon, des hochstapelnden Schwindlers gelten. Shawn agiert den reichen, aber wenig männlichen Rivalen in der Liebe, während Pegeen als junges Mädchen gleichzeitig Ansätze zur eifersüchtigen und scharfzüngigen Xanthippe erkennen läßt. Wiewohl so die Nähe zu gängigen Typen der Komödie unverkennbar ist, reichen solche Zuordnungen für eine Kennzeichnung der Figuren doch nicht aus. Besser kommt ihre Eigenart schon in den Blick, wenn sie als typisch westirische Ausprägungen dieser traditionellen Typen verstanden werden und zusätzlich auch noch ein für Synge wie für andere Autoren der Zeit charakteristischer lebensphilosophischer Hintergrund in Rechnung gestellt wird. Den Obrigkeiten, kirchlichen wie staatlichen, gegenüber sind Synges Westler aufmüpfig und unterwürfig zugleich, wie sie auch ein zwiespältiges Verhältnis zur Gewalt an den Tag legen. Wenn man einmal von dem Feigling Shaneen absieht, der deshalb auch allgemein verachtet wird, begeistern sich alle Figuren an Gewalttaten wie Christys Vatermord oder dem Gattenmord der Witwe Quin oder einem Handgemenge, das einen Polizisten ein Auge gekostet hat. Ja, im Hinblick auf das Treiben beim Begräbnis der alten Kate Cassidy (»there were five men, aye, and six men, stretched out retching speechless on the holy stones«, S. 85) kann man direkt von anarchischen Zügen sprechen, die zunächst im besondern mit Pegeens Vater verknüpft sind, später dann aber stärker auf Christy und seinen Vater übertragen werden. So begründet der Wirt seine Zustimmung zu Pegeens Ehe mit Christy mit den Worten: »I'd liefer face the grave untimely and I seeing a score of grandsons growing up little gallant swearers by the name of God, than go peopling my bedside with puny weeds the like what you'd breed, I'm thinking, out of Shaneen Keogh« (S. 90).

Daß die anarchischen Züge, die Auflehnung gegen die Obrigkeit und die Bewunderung für den Gewalttäter mehr als ein bloßer Jux des Komödienschreibers sind, stellt ein Brief Synges an MacKenna klar: »I think the Law-Maker and the Law-Breaker are both needful in society – as the lively and volcanic forces are needed to make earth's crust habitable [. . .]« (*Collected Letters*, Bd. 1, S. 76). Dahinter stehen lebensphilosophische Anschauungen, die Synges *Playboy* als Werk der beginnenden Moderne ausweisen. So verrät Pegeens Zeitklage (S. 11 f.) und ihr Zögern, einen Shawn zu heiraten, der ihr wie eine Vogelscheuche vorkommt »with no savagery or fine words in him at all« (S. 87), was wir heute Frustration und Unbefriedigtsein nennen würden. Ähnliches gilt in Abwandlung für Sara Tansey, die Christys Schuhe mitgehen lassen will, um endlich einmal eine anständige Sünde beichten zu können, oder die Witwe Quin, die in bester existentialistischer Manier den am Horizont verschwindenden Schiffen nachträumt, »and I thinking on the gallant hairy fellows are drifting beyond, and myself long years living alone« (S. 67). Im Fall des Helden selber ist es die Emanzipation von der Autorität des Vaters, überhaupt das Problem der Selbstwerdung, das ausgesprochen modern wirkt und aus dem Synge solches Kapital für die Komik geschlagen hat. Der Christy, der eingangs in der Wirtsstube erscheint, ist ein junger Mann ohne Selbstvertrauen, zu dem ihm dann die wilden Phantasien seiner ländlichen, besonders weiblichen Bewunderer und nicht minder seine eigenen Ausmalungen im Ablauf einer Komödienhandlung verhelfen. Und zwar ist das Ausspielen der eigenen seelischen Nöte und Bedürfnisse vor der Kulisse eines mitgehenden Publikums – hier also den Dörflern –, das diese Selbstfindung ermöglicht. Die Grundlage für das Zusammenspiel, sozusagen sein rudimentäres Libretto, ist die Illusion von Christys Vatermord in ihren Auswirkungen auf den Protagonisten wie auf sein Publikum. Mit der Entlarvung der Illusion verliert das Geschehen seinen Spielcharakter und Christy seine Rolle, die ihm zur Selbstfindung und zur selbstverständlichen Anerkennung seitens der Mitspieler verholfen hat. Jetzt muß sich zeigen, ob die einmal gewonnene Identität stark genug ist, um sich nach außen hin zu behaupten oder ob sie mit dem Verlust der Spielrolle wieder zerbricht.

Der Christy nun, der seinen Vater in dieser Situation ein zweites Mal niederschlägt, tut dies, um die verlorenen Sympathien Pegeens und der Dörfler wiederzugewinnen, und erreicht doch nur, daß sie sich jetzt endgültig von ihm abwenden, weil ihnen inzwischen der Unterschied zwischen Fiktion und Realität aufgegangen ist. Es ist dies eine Erkenntnis, die längst fällig war und insofern auch noch so etwas wie eine verspätete Ehrenrettung für die Dörfler darstellt. Die Einsicht wird freilich teuer bezahlt: indem sich die Dörfler den Realitäten des Alltags beugen, also etwa aus Angst vor der Justiz Christy ausliefern wollen, verdrängen sie gleichzeitig Teile ihres Wesens, gehören sie zu den »Narren der Erde« (S. 94), die wie Pegeen am Ende ihren verpaßten Möglichkeiten nachtrauern. »Oh, my grief, I've lost him surely. I've lost the only playboy of the western world« (S. 101).

Dem Playboy selber hingegen verhilft die Katastrophe, die Verstoßung durch Pegeen und die Dörfler zur endgültigen Selbstfindung. Er hat nicht nur versucht, seinen Vater zu ermorden, sondern söhnt sich am Schluß auch wieder mit ihm aus, ja, beide beginnen gemeinsam ein neues Leben als Landstreicher. Das mag, oberflächlich gesehen, alles sehr ungereimt klingen und paßt als Schluß zu der Komik des Stücks. Es paßt aber auch noch insofern, als wir hier beim Helden die Folie zu dem Verhalten der Dörfler finden; denn Christys Entscheid für die Existenz des besitzlosen Fahrenden ist ein Entscheid gegen die Zwänge von Zivilisation und Gesellschaft und ein Bekenntnis zu gemeinhin unterdrückten Strebungen der Psyche.

So jedenfalls sah es Synge, der die Briefe an seine Braut, die Schauspielerin Molly Allgood, mit »Your Old Tramp« zu unterschreiben pflegte und einmal bekannte, daß er in seiner Jugend jedes Frühjahr und jeden Herbst einen wilden Drang verspürt habe, »to wander off and tramp the world«. An anderer Stelle sieht er in den Fahrenden einen romantischen Zug und ein Gegenmittel gegen die Wut, mit der man seit Jahrhunderten in Irland nach Landbesitz strebe. Auf dem Hintergrund dieser Anschauungen leuchtet ein, warum Synge den Helden seines *Playboy* wie vorher schon die Heldin in *In the Shadow of the Glen* am Schluß die Existenz eines Fahrenden wählen läßt.

Sprache und Komik

Wie kein anderes Werkelement trägt Synges Sprache zur
Eigenart des Stücks bei, so daß wir die Frage nach der inneren
Form abschließend auf die Sprachgebung und die Komik aus-
dehnen wollen.

Beginnen wir mit einer Eigenart des irischen Englisch, die
Synge aufnimmt und fast bis zum Überdruß häuft: der soge-
nannten »and«-Konstruktion. Wo das Standardenglisch unter-
schiedliche Verbindungswörter einsetzt, Relativpronomina,
begründende, einräumende und andere Konjunktionen mehr,
verwendet Synge nach dem Vorbild des Irischen nur die Konjunktion *and*. Wenn Pegeen im 3. Akt erklärt, daß sie Christy
heiraten wolle, entrüstet und entsetzt sich ihr Vater mit den
Worten: »You'd be making him a son to me and he wet and
crusted with his fathers blood?« (S. 86). Anstelle der losen und
unbestimmten Verknüpfung mit dem »Und« erwartet der
Hörer oder Leser üblicherweise einen strafferen Anschluß, sei
es nun mittels eines Relativpronomens oder gar einer begrün-
denden (da er) oder adversativen Konjunktion (wo er doch).
Just darauf aber, auf ein bloßes Reihen der Dinge und nicht
auf ein Über- und Unterordnen oder logische Eindeutigkeit,
zielt die »and«-Konstruktion ab – und nicht nur diese. Denn in
die gleiche Richtung weisen auch andere Spracheigentümlich-
keiten, etwa der regelmäßige Wegfall des Relativpronomens,
des indirekten Fragepronomens oder – noch auffälliger – die
zahllosen Dubletten vom Typ: »wet and crusted«. Eine Reihe
dieser Dubletten lassen sich auch als rhetorisches Hendiadyoin
bezeichnen, d. h. als Intensivierung e i n e s Begriffs durch
z w e i (synonyme) Ausdrücke. Danach würde Synges »a roar
of rage and astonishment« (S. 77) normalerweise als »a roar of
astonished rage« umschrieben. Das Beispiel zeigt besonders
klar, wie die gängige logische Unterordnung zur gedanklich
unbestimmteren Nebenordnung wird, ein Zug der sich nicht
minder an Synges Katalogen mit ihren häufig inkongruenten
Zusammenstellungen beobachten läßt. Hinter all dem, den
»and«-Konstruktionen, den Auslassungen von Pronomina,

den Dubletten und Katalogen, kurz dem Zug zur bloßen Reihung steht der Glaube, den wir nicht nur bei Synge finden, daß eine solche Sprachgebung »ursprünglicher«, weil eben vorrational, ist.

Ob nun ursprünglich oder nicht, unbestritten ist, daß Synges Sprache unerhört anschaulich und lebendig wirkt. Es ist dies ein Vorzug, den nahezu alle Kritiker hervorgehoben haben, wenn freilich auch im gleichen Atemzug gern von Redundanz gesprochen wird und davon, daß Synge in der Redseligkeit seiner Figuren die irische Untugend des »blather«, des leeren Geschwätzes, aufs Korn nehme. Besonders auffällig im Hinblick auf die Redundanz sind Synges Genitivattribute, an denen sich stellvertretend der Zusammenhang mit der Anschaulichkeit studieren läßt. Der folgende Satz, mit dem Mike auf den Entschluß seiner Tochter, den Vatermörder Christy zu heiraten, reagiert, enthält neben einer Dublette zwei der für Synge so charakteristischen Genitivattribute: »Oh, aren't you a heathen daughter to go shaking the fat of my heart, and I swamped and drownded with the weight of drink?« (S. 87). Wo üblicherweise eine schlichte Aussage wie »shake my heart« oder »drownded with drink« zu erwarten wäre, fügt Synge fast regelmäßig eine »logisch« unnötige Erweiterung ein. Freilich geht es ihm weniger um Logik als um eine schon fast handfest zu nennende Sinnenhaftigkeit, ganz zu schweigen von der damit verknüpften Komik. Was da durch die unchristliche Tochter gerüttelt und erschüttert wird, ist nicht einfach das Herz – so könnte der Ausdruck noch als blasses Klischee wirken und nicht wirklich zu Herzen gehen –, nein, es ist das Fett, das Beste vom Herzen, das da so handgreiflich vor dem geistigen Auge des Hörers ersteht, daß er es wie einen Wackelpudding vor sich sieht. Ähnlich sieht der Hörer in der Einbildung förmlich, wie durch das herabziehende Gewicht des Trunks das Ich überschwemmt worden und untergegangen ist. Das Beispiel zeigt, daß Synges vielgerühmte Anschaulichkeit (ganz im Sinn der rhetorischen Energeia) den Zuschauer oder Leser über ein Phantasiebild, ein sinnenhaftes Vor-Augen-Stellen in seinen Bann schlägt.

Die gleiche Kunst der Illusionierung, die wir am Beispiel der für Synge so auffälligen Genitivattribute erläutert haben, hätte sich im übrigen ebenso gut an andern Stilfiguren, etwa den Dubletten oder Katalogen oder an übergreifenden Texteinheiten wie etwa Christys Ausmalungen seiner Heldentat vorführen lassen. Groß ist auch die Versuchung, von einer Fiktionalisierung der Realität zu sprechen, doch beruht eine solche Deutung auf der irrigen Annahme, daß die Realität der Sprache vorausliege und den Maßstab für deren Wahrheitsgehalt abgebe. Dagegen spricht, daß alle Versuche, aus den Ausmalungen Christys oder auch denen seines Vaters den genauen Hergang des Mordversuchs zu rekonstruieren, Stückwerk bleiben. Um es an einem Detail zu veranschaulichen: empört weist Christy Pegeens Vorstellung zurück, er habe sich zu Haus wie ein König von Norwegen oder ein morgenländischer Potentat gefühlt: »The like of a king, is it! And I after toiling, moiling, digging, dodging from the dawn till dusk with never a sight of joy or sport [. . .]« (S. 32). Soweit Christy selber! Und nun, was der Vater später über seinen Sohn zu berichten weiß: »[. . .] he a lier on walls, a talker of folly, a man you'd see stretched the half of the day in the brown ferns with his belly to the sun« (S. 63). Die Frage, die sich aufzudrängen scheint, welche der beiden Darstellungen stimme oder doch der Wahrheit näherkomme, ist gleichwohl verkehrt gestellt, weil beide Sprecher keinen Faktenbericht geben, sondern emotional getönte Meinungen und Stimmungen äußern. Wie die Zustände auf dem väterlichen Hof wirklich waren, erfahren wir aus Christys Darstellung nicht, sondern nur, wie ihm zumute war. In der Verallgemeinerung aber bedeutet das: die Figuren agieren und artikulieren unbefriedigte Sehnsüchte, Hoffnungen und Ängste, Haß- und Rachegefühle, aber natürlich auch Hochgestimmtheit, Niedergeschlagenheit und andere Affekte mehr. Hinzu kommt, daß sie aufeinander reagieren, daß sie ihre Worte und Handlungen auf ihre Gesprächspartner und ihr Publikum abstellen. Dieser zweite Aspekt läßt sich besonders anschaulich an der Szene im 2. Akt studieren, in der Christy den Mädchen und der Witwe Quin seine Heldentat zum besten gibt. Die Bewunderung der Frauen beflügelt nicht nur die Phantasie des Erzählers, wenn er das Geschehen in der Erinnerung schrecklich-schön und in bis dahin unerreichter Eindringlichkeit ausmalt; gerissen spannt er auch die Neugier und die Ungeduld seiner Zuhörer auf die Folter, indem er die Tat bis zum Gehtnichtmehr hinauszögert. Spätestens an diesem Punkt werden wir dann freilich auch auf die Regie des Autors Synge verwiesen, der letztlich darüber entscheidet, welche Affekte eine Figur bewegen und wie sie in einer bestimmten Situation auf ihre Partner eingeht.

Nicht minder hat der Autor seine Hand bei der Komik des Werks im Spiel. Und da der *Playboy* auf weite Strecken ein Rededrama ist, wollen wir für die Komik stellvertretend auf Synges Klischees und schmückende Beiwörter eingehen, die wir bei der Behandlung seiner vielgerühmten Anschaulichkeit bislang ausgeklammert haben. Klischee und Anschaulichkeit bilden in Synges Sprache keine sich ausschließenden Gegensätze, sondern gehen Hand in Hand, oder – anders ausgedrückt – dem Zug zur Illusionierung des Publikums wohnt auch noch ein Zug zur Desillusionierung inne, und beide zusammen machen die Komik des Ganzen aus. Sehen wir uns daraufhin noch einmal ein Stückchen Dialog an. Bevor Christy nicht mehr ein noch aus weiß und seinen Vater zum zweiten Mal niederschlägt, hat er versucht, den Alten zur Gnade zu bewegen. Und zwar fragt er, was den Vater dazu treibe, ihn zu quälen, »when I'd ask the thunders of the might of God to blast me if I ever did hurt to any saving only that one single blow« (S. 92).

Das lammfromme Eingeständnis einer Missetat, wenn auch nur einer einzigen, nimmt sich gering aus nach den gewaltigen Donnerkeilen des göttlichen Strafgerichts, verfängt aber trotzdem nicht bei dem Opfer. Lärmend hält der Alte dagegen, daß wenn Christy so wenig getan habe, er halt ein Taugenichts sei – und ob denn zu bestreiten sei, daß nicht gerade diese Sorte alle Sünden der Welt auf dem Kerbholz hätte: »If you didn't, you're a poor good-for-nothing, and isn't it by the like of you the sins of the whole world are committed?« (S. 92). Was

Vater und Sohn hier bravourös vorführen, ist ein Scheinge-
fecht, bei dem es Christy darauf ankommt, aus der Not eine
Tugend zu machen, der Alte aber auf Kosten seines Sohnes
seine eigene Haut rettet. Uns freilich mutet die Szene als Spiel
an, als Wettstreit zwischen zwei ländlichen Sophisten, denen
kein moralisches und religiöses Klischee zu heilig und kein
Wortspiel zu billig ist, wenn es darum geht, dem andern den
Schwarzen Peter zuzuschieben. Ja, aller Scheinlogik und allen
Klischees zum Trotz erscheinen gerade diese gängigen Orien-
tierungs- und Wertmaßstäbe der Alltagssprache hier in Frage
gestellt, halten sich Logik und Unsinn, Tugend und Opportunismus die Waage. Zwielichtig sind viele Reden im *Playboy*,
wie auch ein Blick auf die Vielzahl der schmückenden Beiwörter zeigen kann. Wenn Pegeen an ihren Vater herantritt, um
den Vatermörder Christy zu heiraten, schimpft der Wirt sie
zunächst eine »heidnische Tochter« (S. 87), bevor er sich dann
in seinem Ehesegen anschickt, den Bund der beiden zu vertei-
digen. Das Adjektiv »heidnisch« individualisiert hier nicht,
sondern typisiert und wertet, und zwar auf höchst fragwürdige
Weise, indem es die Menschen in Christen und Heiden einteilt,
so wie der alte Mahon in unserm vorigen Beispiel mit einer
ähnlich pauschalen Unterscheidung zwischen Tugendhaften
und Taugenichtsen operiert hatte.

Nach dem Muster der »heidnischen Tochter« funktionieren
auch die andern schmückenden Adjektive, die auf Schritt und
Tritt im *Playboy* begegnen; um nur ein paar der denkwürdig-
sten zu nennen: Pegeens berühmtes Paar von der schneidigen
Geschichte und der schmutzigen Tat oder Christys Bild von
der Sonne, die zwischen den Wolken und dem Hügel hervor-
tritt, »and it shining green in my face« (S. 48). Diese stehenden
Beiwörter typisieren, und indem sie typisieren, legen sie eine
Wertung nahe, die ihre Fragwürdigkeit gleichzeitig verhüllt
und enthüllt und damit zum Lachen reizt. Analog posaunen
die zahlreichen vollmundigen moralischen und christlichen
Sprüche den blanken Opportunismus und den Eigennutz aus,
den sie eigentlich verschweigen wollen, und es ergibt sich als
Gesamtbefund, daß die sauberen Trennungen zwischen Logik

und Unsinn, zwischen Moral und Unmoral, Fiktion und Realität, auf die sich die zivilisierte Welt so viel einbildet, in Synges komischer Welt des irischen Westens aufgehoben sind.

Eben deswegen billigt Synge dieser ein größeres Maß an Ursprünglichkeit zu. Mit einer einseitigen Verherrlichung dieser ursprünglichen Welt hat das freilich wenig zu tun, wie Synges Widersacher im Lager der Nationalisten schon zu Recht erkannt haben. Synge selber freilich hat die Komik nicht gestört; er sah in der Mischung aus »Freude« und »Wirklichkeit«, von denen das Vorwort zum *Playboy* spricht, vielmehr gerade ein Bekenntnis zum Leben.

Rainer Lengeler

Inhalt